CONTENTS

When I presented the *Women Mean Business* television series in 1990, women returners were big news. Now, a year later, they have dropped from the headlines and recession is in the news. But the longer term predictions are that employers will still find it hard to recruit skilled staff. If woman returners are going to make the most of job opportunities then they need good advice more than ever.

While filming the series I met many women who inspired me with their courage and determination – women from all walks of life who were embarking on new careers or picking up old ones. This book tells their stories.

So, if you are thinking of returning to paid work or taking a course *Women Mean Business* will help you to do this. So read on!

Glenda Jackson.

INTRODUCTION

In an ideal world, I would like advice and information on every aspect of returning to paid work. That is, childcare, careers, courses, companies, what to ask for at interviews, how to manage the financial side of returning and how to deal with my own feelings of guilt about leaving the children.

At the moment I don't know where or how to start – which order do I do things in? I can't arrange my childcare until I've got a job and know how much I'm earning, and I can't accept a job until I know my children will be cared for.

I need some signposts, some leads about which organisations offer what sort of help. I'd like to know what the Job Centre offers and where I can find someone who will sit down and talk to me, and how I can find out which companies are going to help women returners.

Most people have heard of the threatened skills shortage. As the numbers of school leavers fall, employers will be looking to other groups to take jobs that school and college leavers have traditionally filled. So the 1990s is a good time to be a woman returning to paid work. You should find that there are more and better opportunities for you to return to work than there were ten or even five years ago. It is predicted that all sectors of the economy are going to face shortages of skilled people in the next 10 years, and clerical staff, sales staff, machinists, computing personnel and engineers are among the groups that are in short supply now.

For too long, women, and other disadvantaged groups in society, have been 'ghettoised' in a limited range of jobs. Women have tended to work in jobs in the service sector, in cleaning and catering for example, and in the caring professions such as nursing and teaching. Now, there is a chance that this will change. If employers are going to fill their vacancies then they are going to have to spread their recruitment net more widely, which means conditions of employment should improve as employers are forced to work harder to keep their staff. Women returners will be needed, not only to work as shop assistants to cover the Christmas rush, or to provide emergency night-time nursing cover in hospitals, or as supply teachers when the class teacher falls ill, but to fill secure jobs that offer regular hours, pension schemes and chances of training and promotion.

The 1990s could see much greater equality in the workforce and women's skills and talents being used where they have been wasted before. The employment climate is becoming more 'woman friendly' as employers recognise the need to recruit and retain more women staff. They are reviewing their recruitment and employment practices with women returners in mind. The Inland Revenue, for example, offers flexitime. Many local authorities offer job-sharing. Dixons Stores Group offers a term-time-only working arrangement and International Computers Limited employ computer staff who work from home.

But while the chance *should* be there for women returners to get jobs and to get better jobs, it is very hard to know where to start. How do you try and make the most of the opportunities on offer? Is there someone who can give you advice? What courses are available and how much do they cost? How do you find out about job vacancies? How do you apply? Could you possibly set up in business on your own?

We hope that this book will help you to answer each of

these questions. Once you have taken the first steps and chosen a course, applied for a job, or perhaps started planning to set up in business on your own, it will help to prepare you for the next stage. It gives advice on how to make the most of a training course, how to perform well at interview, how to get off to a good start in a new job, and how to draw up a viable business plan and start to trade. It also explains new measures which are being introduced by employers and which could benefit you – bringing more flexible ways of working that enable women to combine home and work responsibilities with less stress.

The book begins by looking at that all-important area of confidence. Nothing saps confidence like being out of a paid job. Low self-confidence is a huge barrier for women. It makes us undervalue ourselves and our potential. It holds us back from seeking out opportunities and from making the most of our lives. We hope that this book will help you to build up your confidence. The first chapter contains a number of confidence-building exercises and strategies. Other chapters often refer to the use you can make of the many skills you have learnt in your time at home. By spending time caring for children and running a home you have more to offer an employer, not less. Being a mother is more demanding, challenging and skilful than many paid jobs and it will have given you a level of maturity and understanding of people that little else can.

We also hope that this book will make the world of work seem a little less alien. Even a short time away can make women feel like outsiders. Included in the book are lots of quotes from women who have returned. They talk about how they made decisions about courses and jobs, what it feels like to return to paid work, how they plan and manage their lives and how they have made the most of new opportunities. We have also included information about how employment practices have changed, for example, with the introduction of new technologies and equal opportunities policies.

We hope too that you will feel encouraged by this book to see further help and advice. In particular, you may need to talk to a local expert – such as someone from careers guidance – to find out what jobs are available in the area where you live. For while there will be a general skills shortage, this will not be evenly spread across the UK, and there may not be a wide range of job vacancies just where *you* happen to live.

Finally, we hope that even if you are initially unsuccessful in your efforts to return to work, you won't give up. Most people don't get the first job they apply for, and it is only those who stick at it and who learn from past failures, who get the jobs in the end.

ABOUT THIS BOOK

Here is a summary of the main subjects that each chapter covers so you can read the chapters that interest you most.

Chapter 1 *Women and Confidence* – In this chapter we look at why women tend to suffer from low self-confidence and suggest a number of exercises and strategies that will help to build up your confidence.

Chapter 2 *Education and Training* – This chapter will help you through the maze of education and training opportunities which are available for adults. It explains where you can go for advice about courses, it describes the kinds of courses that are on offer and it looks at the education and training opportunities that are available in the areas of employment that are currently being hit by skills shortages. The chapter also indicates the cost of courses and explains what grants and bursaries are available.

Chapter 3 *Getting a Job* – This chapter covers the whole process of trying to get a job, from tracking down job vacancies to preparing for interview. It suggests ways of making the most of the skills and abilities you have and discusses how to fill in application forms and draw up a CV. It looks at changes in employment procedures such as the equal opportunities legislation, and it discusses ways for you to ensure that your family and friends support you in your efforts to find paid work.

Chapter 4 *Starting a Job* – This chapter gives advice on how to survive, and enjoy, those first few hectic weeks at work. It suggests ways of coping with stress and includes strategies for managing your time. It explores the ways that relationships change when women return to work, and recommends joining a discussion group of other returners for an invaluable source of support.

Chapter 5 *Childcare* – Here we look at the most difficult problem that many women returners face – finding good childcare. The chapter explores what is available both for pre-school and school-age children and explains how you can find out about what is available. If you can find nothing which is suitable, it describes how you can go about recruiting a carer yourself. It also looks at how to judge whether a particular person or place is a good choice for your child, and suggests ways of helping your childcare to work well.

Chapter 6 *New Ways to Work* – This chapter is about ways of making the hours you work more flexible, arranging them to suit you. It looks at part-time work, flexitime, job-sharing, term-time working, and homeworking or teleworking. It gives advice on how to seek these alternatives out, and how to ask for them if they are not available. It also looks at the pros and cons of the different arrangements you can make.

Chapter 7 *Working for Yourself* – Working for yourself is the fastest growing sector of the economy and more and more women are choosing to set up on their own. This chapter describes the first steps that you would need to take to go into business. It begins by encouraging you to explore why you want to work for yourself, because the clearer you are about this, the better your chance of success. It then suggests ways that you can assess your skills and talents. It gives advice on coming up with a business idea and explains how to do market research. In addition, it describes how to find and make the best use of business advice and training opportunities. There is also some brief advice on how to write a business plan.

KEEPING ABREAST OF THE CHANGES

All the details in this book are correct at the time of writing. However, the situation with courses, recruitment policy, employment law and, especially, financial law relating to the setting up of new businesses are all areas subject to constant change. So it is important to keep abreast of the changes by talking to experts and advisers to ensure that you get the information that you want and need to achieve your goals.

CHAPTER

ONE

WOMEN &
CONFIDENCE

LIZ BARGH

Liz Bargh has been a woman returner twice – the first time was after her daughter was born and the second after she completed her degree in Economics.

Her work has always been in the field of Personnel and for the past 12 years she has been involved in equal opportunities with particular focus on women returners. She was head of the Pepperell Unit from 1988 to 1990 when she joined the Domino Consultancy as a Director.

INTRODUCTION

I get so nervous at the very thought of going back to work – everything has changed so much and I've done nothing for ten years.

Confidence isn't a gift that some people have and others don't. It is a combination of attitudes and behaviour which can be learned and improved on, like any other skill. Becoming confident is within the grasp of each of us. Every woman who has been out of the workforce in order to care for a family will have experienced some loss of confidence. For some women, this can be acute; for others it is easily regained. This chapter aims to help you rebuild the confidence you have lost. It contains lots of exercises to help you to work out your strengths and to overcome your weaknesses. In particular, the exercises will help you to identify the skills that you have developed while you have been away from paid work, and that will prove invaluable when you do return.

To most of us the word 'confident' describes other people, never ourselves. Women, particularly, are amazed when others say they appear confident. Whatever their outside appearance they know that inside they are a quivering bundle of nerves and fears.

Of course this is not a feeling solely confined to women. Men experience crises of confidence, but in general they appear to be able to maintain a higher level of self-confidence than women. Or, at the very least, they are able to disguise the feelings of self-doubt more effectively than women. Confidence is, therefore, often seen as a much greater issue for women than for men.

Where does this lack of confidence come from? Women are exposed to different social expectations from men. Little girls are praised for being pretty, conforming to stereotypes such as 'sugar and spice and all things nice'. As we grow up we are expected to become beautiful, slim, perfect wives and mothers. But what happens if we achieve none of these things? We feel guilty! Guilt is probably the biggest enemy of confidence, because feeling guilty implies a sense of failure and we cannot feel confident if we are in some way failing.

These feelings of low self-confidence are exacerbated when we leave paid work. We live in a society that values paid employment above any other form of work. Even if we leave to do something that society should value just as much, such as to look after children or an elderly relative, we find that we are valued less.

Leaving a paid job also leads to a loss of identity. People in paid jobs can always define themselves by what they do: 'I'm a nurse'; 'I'm a teacher'; or 'I'm a computer operator'. But when we leave paid work, we lose this way of defining ourselves. Instead, we are often only known in terms of our relationship to another person – as someone's wife or mother or daughter, and not as a person in our own right. And as we lose a clear sense of our own identity, we also rapidly lose touch with the world of work. It is amazing how quickly work becomes like a foreign land, so that the thought of returning, even after a few months, can feel very daunting.

We also lose confidence because we lose financial independence. For many women, this means having no money to spend on themselves at all. It also means having to rely on someone or something else – on a partner or on the state – to provide for us, taking away the dignity that we feel when we are able to provide for ourselves.

WHAT HAPPENS TO US
WHEN WE LOSE CONFIDENCE?

The first thing that we do is we begin to devalue what we can do. Perhaps this is the most damaging aspect of loss of confidence. We begin to believe that the things that we can do are things that anyone can do. The consequence of this is that we believe that we have nothing to offer anyone. We assume that everyone can do the things that we can do and, what is more, they can do them better.

> *I see all these high-powered women in the magazines and on television – they make it all look so easy. I can't even keep the house tidy from one day to the next.*

The second thing that we do is we fear failure. When we lack confidence we tend to avoid putting ourselves in situations in which we could make mistakes. We worry disproportionately about how other people will see us, and we do not take risks. Consequently we tend to limit the opportunities open to us and we undersell ourselves.

We also worry about fitting into a work environment and having to learn new skills. Questions arise such as 'how will I manage to cope with new technology?' or 'what should I wear?' The possibility of working with colleagues who are much younger than yourself, managing the balance of home and work, and making sure that everything gets done are yet further areas which cause concern and anxiety.

If we take all these worries and add all the effects of loss of confidence together, it is not surprising that returning to work can be a very nerve-racking prospect. Asking yourself questions like: 'What sort of work do I want to do?', 'What can I do?'; 'How do I find a job?'; 'What should I do and say at interview?' all help to contribute to the feeling that no one would want to employ you anyway. Often this feeling becomes self-fulfilling and the lack of confidence becomes reinforced.

MAKING A START

In this chapter, we will describe four steps on the road to regaining confidence. The first is to decide what it is that you really want from life. What are your goals and what are your priorities? We are bombarded by other people telling us what we want. Every magazine shows us the sort of life-style we ought to be aiming for. They feature women who appear to be able to combine highly satisfying careers with happy family life. They show us models wearing clothes that would look distinctly out of place in the everyday lives that most of us lead.

It is important to recognise that you can achieve all sorts of things in your life and magazines give us a lot of very good examples of women who have done this. But the most important thing is to know what *your* goals and priorities are – not what other people expect of you – and what you want for yourself.

The second step is to take stock of yourself. What are your strengths? What are your weaknesses? Most women are only too aware of their weaknesses, but are unable to recognise their strengths. It is important to get to know your strengths so that you can build on them and decide which of your weaknesses you wish to try and overcome.

The third step is to identify the opportunities that are open to you and the difficulties you face. Often our confidence gets knocked when the difficulties seem overwhelming, and this means that we may miss opportunities that were there all the time.

The fourth step is to take action. This includes employing strategies that you can use every day to help you feel and look confident, and drawing up an action plan of the things to do in order to reach your goals. This is the most important stage in rebuilding your confidence. The actions you take may be very simple, but the process of doing something positive gives you a sense of control that helps you to feel more confident about tackling something bigger.

You are now about to start the journey to meet the 'confident you'. These are the steps that you will take along the way:

● Setting goals and priorities that are right for *you*
● Weighing up your strengths and weaknesses
● Identifying opportunities and difficulties or threats
● Taking action – simple steps you can take, and drawing up an action plan to help you reach your goals.

1 SETTING YOUR OWN GOALS AND PRIORITIES

Just knowing some of the things that I don't want to do has helped me to decide what my priorities are and what steps I should take.

Many women find it very difficult to set goals and priorities for themselves. We are used to putting other people's wants and needs before our own, and many of us have been brought up to believe that if we put ourselves before others, we are being selfish. Our role in the family reinforces this belief and we put our children and partners first. The majority of us choose to do this and would be unhappy to do otherwise.

The difficulty is to recognise that sometimes we need to take account of our own goals and priorities and that whilst it may not be desirable to put them first, it is important to consider them alongside those of others. We can then negotiate or discuss whose needs will take priority at any given time. There is no magic formula that will answer everyone's needs, but taking these steps will help:

- Know yourself. What are your goals, what is important to you? What are your strengths? What are your weaknesses?
- Like yourself. Look at yourself in the mirror and say, 'I'm OK. Maybe I'm not perfect and I'm going to get better, but basically I like what I am.' After all, how can anyone else like you if you do not like yourself?
- Be yourself. Too often we try to be something or someone we are not. That creates stress and will probably not work anyway.

It is important to start setting yourself goals. Some of us can see very clearly what we want to achieve and where we want to go. But for many of us, there appear to be very big boulders in the way which are blocking our path. Others have difficulty in seeing anything at all. It is as if we are surrounded by a thick fog. Some of us can see where we want to be, but cannot identify which path to take. As our confidence builds we can begin to see how to overcome these obstacles and we can begin to make plans to achieve our goals. But first we need to identify what our goals are.

LOOKING BACK AT WHAT YOU HAVE DONE

In order to look ahead, it may be helpful first to look at what you have achieved so far in your life. Each and every one of us has done a certain amount already that we can feel proud of. What are some of the things that you have done that you feel good about?

Your life-long experiences make you the person you are today. Experiences add to our knowledge and from each experience we learn a whole new set of skills. Below is a list of common life-experiences. How many of them have you had? Tick each one that you have coped with or experienced and add any others that are not on the list.

Moving house	Getting married
Getting divorced	Caring for children
Caring for the elderly	Personal injury
Organising a special event	Financial problems
Death of someone close	Travel
Coping with a disability	Living alone
Family problems	Personal problems

All of these are quite momentous experiences which, if they happened to you, you probably just got on and coped with. But 'just coping' is quite an achievement in itself, and we should feel proud that we have managed to come through stressful and difficult times. And in the process, we will have used a variety of skills that we may not recognise and value. We will have used skills with people, such as persuading an unwilling child to go to school, or negotiating the best way to resolve a family crisis. We will have used planning or organising skills, such as budgeting to ease financial hardship, or planning which route to take when travelling. And we will have used skills with machines, such as learning to use household equipment, or a home computer.

LOOKING AHEAD TO WHAT
YOU WOULD LIKE TO DO

The following exercise will help you to start thinking about your life goals. You will need to find a quiet place and to be undisturbed for ten minutes or so.

Sit back comfortably, and relax. Imagine that you are going on a journey and that you are travelling through time. You are moving forward ten years in time. You are arriving at your home ten years from now. Stop and look around you. Open your front door and go inside. How many rooms are there?; who is living with you in your home?; what ages are they? Now you are leaving your home and going to work. You arrive at your place of work. What sort of organisation is it?; is it big?; is it small?; what is your role in the organisation? Now you are going to a party. It is in celebration of something you have achieved in the past ten years. What have you achieved during these years? What is the celebration for?

You are now travelling back in time to the present. Write down three key things that you saw on your journey.

Some people find it very hard to project forward ten years, but it is important to start the process of planning. It may well be that your plans will change over time. After all, no one can accurately predict what will happen in the future. But this process does help you to identify your priorities.

2 WEIGHING UP YOUR STRENGTHS AND WEAKNESSES

While having a sense of where we are trying to go will help to build our confidence, it is also vital to take a stock check of our skills and abilities and our weaknesses too. Have you ever taken stock of your skills? Few of us have. We are brought up to believe that to acknowledge that we are good at something is to boast. As a result, we are usually much better at talking about the things we can't do than about the things we can. But this doesn't help us when we go for an interview for a job, for example. After all, which prospective employer wants to hear about our weaknesses!

It is very important to be able to talk realistically about your strengths – the things you are good at – to be able to say to yourself 'yes, that is something I do well'. This not only helps to build your confidence, but also helps you to plan which direction you want to take in your future career and your life generally. It is much more productive to build on the things you do well than to struggle constantly to develop skills that are difficult for you. This is not to say that we should give up easily and that we should not bother to try to learn new things. It is more about recognising that there are some things that do not come naturally to us – these could be described as our weaknesses – and that while it may be necessary to overcome them, they will never be things that we want to put all our energy into. We need to build on our strengths and minimise our weaknesses.

DRAWING A BRICK WALL

So how do we start? Let us look, first of all, at our strengths. Take a sheet of paper and draw a brick wall. Imagine that the very bottom layer of bricks represents your basic qualifications – any exam that you have passed, or any certificate that you have received that qualifies you to do anything. It might be a City and Guilds certificate in catering or an RSA certificate in typing or a CSE pass, or it could be a driving licence or a swimming certificate. Whatever it is, put it down.

The next layer of bricks represents your skills. It is often very difficult to identify what our skills are. After all many of us have never been encouraged to do so. Basically your skills are the things that you do well. Do not worry if you feel you cannot do anything! Many women feel the same and it is not true. Doing this exercise will help you to realise that you have many more skills than you were aware of.

Gill, for example, organises the annual door-to-door collection for the Red Cross in her neighbourhood. To do this successfully, she has to use a number of skills – skills that she did not know that she had. She had to get to know her local area well so that she could divide it into manageable-sized chunks. She had to persuade people to carry out collections within their own area, encourage them to complete the collections within a set time, and then had to collect the money in from all her helpers and account for it all. She found that she was using all kinds of skills and as she became aware of this, so her confidence grew.

TASKS YOU PERFORM

Take a sheet of paper and write down the main tasks you perform every day. These may include cooking the family meals, doing the shopping, taking and collecting the children from school, washing and cleaning. If you do any voluntary work, write down the main tasks you perform for the organisation you are involved with as well. You may be responsible for organising the annual jumble sale, or the summer outing for elderly people, or for helping with the Parent Teachers Association.

Spend some time writing down all the tasks that you can think of that you carry out.

SKILLS YOU USE

Now think of the skills you use in order to do the tasks effectively. For example, think of cooking a meal. What do you have to do to get a meal for four people ready on time? You have to prepare and plan the ingredients and utensils that you will need. You have to buy the food and probably budget carefully. You have to organise and plan the timing to ensure that everything is ready at the right time. You have to be able to carry out a number of tasks at the same time in order to put all the different dishes on the table at once. (How many of you have families where half eat one thing and the other half eat something completely different?) On top of all this you are probably doing a number of other things as well.

So what skills are you using? Time management, organisational skills, financial planning skills, creativity, flexibility and the ability to handle a number of complex tasks at the same time.

SKILLS ARE TRANSFERABLE

The important thing is to recognise that these are highly prized skills in the workplace and that not everyone has them! In fact many of the skills that women gain through their upbringing and experience are directly transferable into the workplace and what is more they are skills that are being identified more and more by employers as essential management skills. Carry on listing your skills and if you get stuck ask your friends what they see as your key skills and what they think you are good at. You will probably find that they cluster under the following headings.

SKILLS WITH PEOPLE

This is one area where women are said to excel. Being a good listener; communicating; negotiating; counselling. These are some of the skills you use every day in the family – sorting out your children's squabbles, listening to your partner's problems at work, deciding which members of your family you will spend Christmas with this year, and so on.

PLANNING/ORGANISING SKILLS

Some of these have already been listed above. But you can probably add others, such as delegating, setting priorities, co-ordinating tasks. Delegating tasks around the family gives us more time to concentrate on the things that are important to us and allows us to set priorities. It is also essential once you return to work. Do not try to be superwoman by attempting to do everything you did when you were at home full-time. Inevitably some things will have to be delegated to other members of the family.

WORKING WITH MACHINES

Most of us today have had to get to grips with new technology and machines and yet this is an area of anxiety for many women planning to return to work. How will you cope with the new technology? Just look around the home and count up the number of machines using new technology. If you are someone who does not understand how to turn the video on, then practise when no one else is around. Do not be put off by the family saying 'Oh, for goodness sake don't be so stupid'. They have had to learn too. And, contrary to popular opinion, it is never too late to learn new skills. One woman went back to work as a secretary in a large computer firm. She had no qualifications other than her secretarial ones, but she decided that she *really wanted* to work on the technical side of the business. She persuaded her boss to allow her to join a graduate training programme for new entrants to the company and now she is happily working all day with computers. She was 50 years old when she changed track and trained with young people half her age.

IDENTIFYING YOUR ACHIEVEMENTS

Let's get back to the brick wall. By now you will have written down the whole range of your skills.

The next stage is to recognise your *achievements*. This is the top layer of your wall and represents the ways in which you have put your skills into practice. Concentrate on those skills which you believe to be your best. Write down at least

two examples of situations when you were able to use those skills. Use full sentences rather than just a couple of words. Here are two examples:

> I am good at managing money. Last year, by careful budgeting I was able to afford to send my son on the school trip for the first time. It meant a lot to him.

> I am good at listening to people. Earlier this year my best friend's husband died and I was able to help her, simply by listening to her when she needed support.

Notice that in both these examples the person has been very positive in the way in which she has described how she has used her skills and in what she has achieved. Try to write down as many examples for yourself as you can. Use positive language and avoid words like 'quite' or 'fairly' so that in future instead of saying, 'well, I am quite good at . . .' you say 'I am good at . . .'.

Read out loud what you have written to a friend or someone in your family. Better still, get them to do the same exercise and practice together until you feel confident at saying what you are good at.

It is important to let other people know about your strengths and abilities when you are thinking about returning to work. Application forms and CVs are often the first opportunity an employer has to find out what you can do and it is important not to undersell yourself. This applies at interviews as well. So, work on your brick wall, and get your friends to help you, until you feel confident that you have skills which are valued in the workplace.

ADDRESSING THE WEAKNESSES

Now you have completed your brick wall. Look at it carefully and you will see that in many parts it is very strong, but in others it may need some repair or adding to. These, if you like, are your weaknesses. Perhaps it would help to build your confidence if you brushed up on some of your skills. Perhaps you would like to gain an extra qualification or to get more training. Or you might have decided by now that you want to retrain for a totally different job from the one you were doing before your break.

All of us have our weak spots and we need to be able to identify them in order to plan for the future we want. But don't be tricked into the pitfall of saying to yourself 'Oh, I'm no good at that, so it's not worth my while trying to do it', because we can find ways of overcoming our weaknesses, either by taking trouble to address them or by minimising their effect.

At school Sally was always bottom of the class in maths. She left school convinced that she was innumerate and for years avoided any job that required working with figures. Eventually she decided that she wanted to study for a degree. On being told that she needed O-level maths in order to enter the college she gave up. It was only the persistence of her husband and a college lecturer that persuaded her to try to study for the required maths exam. Six months later she gained an A-grade in maths. Overcoming that particular hurdle gave Sally confidence to tackle anything.

Look back at your list of things that are hindering you from getting where you want to be. How many of them can you begin to change into strengths?

3 IDENTIFYING OPPORTUNITIES AND DIFFICULTIES

Now you have assessed your strengths and identified your weaknesses it is time to move on and look at opportunities that are open to you and difficulties and barriers you might face. These will depend on your personal circumstances, on what your goals are, and on the particular location in which you live. You will need to take advice too. While opportunities for women returning to paid work have increased in the UK as a whole, local opportunities vary enormously. The next chapter, *Education and Training*, contains information on where to go for local advice.

Let's look at some of the possible opportunities, difficulties and barriers that may face you. Perhaps in your town people are facing redundancy because a large employer is laying people off. What opportunities does this create? How can you overcome the difficulties a situation like this presents?

It is likely that if people are being made redundant some of them will be seeking to set up their own small businesses and may need part-time help. While the large employer may be cutting back, a number of smaller firms may be starting up and very often these can present opportunities for women returning to work.

Anne, who is now the managing director of an engineering company in the West Midlands, started working with the company when it was first set up. It was her first job after being at home with her family and initially she worked a few hours a week. As the firm grew, so did her responsibilities and she took an increasingly responsible role in the company until she took up her present post as managing director.

You may find this exercise helpful. Take a piece of paper and write down on one side of the page all the opportunities that are open to you and on the other side of the page all the difficulties facing you. Between them list your goals. An example is given below:

Opportunities	Goals	Threats
Head office of major insurance company relocates to your area	To become a personal assistant	Poor local transport would make it difficult to collect children from school

The important thing is to build on the opportunities and try to reduce the threats as far as possible. It is also important to weigh up how much you are prepared to give in order to get the job you want. One woman may be prepared to commute to her nearest large city in order to develop her career, whilst another would consider that much too high a price to pay.

4 TAKING ACTION

By following the steps outlined in this chapter, you have begun to take action. Already you are beginning to make things happen. The time you have at home is a golden opportunity to start to put things into place and to prepare for the future.

One step that you could take is to enrol for an education or training course. Chapter two gives information on the kinds of courses that are available, including special courses designed for women who wish to return to paid work.

There are lots of other ways that you can brush up on or develop new skills too. Local organisations always need people to help them and there are always opportunities open to people willing to volunteer. Choose activities that will help you develop particular skills – managing people, book-keeping or fund-raising, for example.

LOOK GOOD, FEEL GOOD

We all know that when we look good we feel good. The only problem is that, when our confidence is low, we do not always recognise that we actually *look good*.

How do you respond to being complimented on your appearance? Do you shuffle and feel embarrassed and say something like 'Oh, really I look a mess . . .' Practice responding positively the next time you are complimented. Look the person in the eyes, smile and say, 'Thank you, I appreciate you saying that . . .' Learning to give and accept compliments will help you to build your confidence.

What is it about your appearance that makes you feel good? Think about it and write it down. One woman always feels better when she has her hair highlighted – when it is darker she feels mousy and dull; when it is lighter she feels brighter and more positive. Our appearance not only influences the way we feel but also the way that others see us. Often we are judged on our appearance, however unfair that may seem. The colours we wear, the clothes we choose, the care we take with our appearance, all make a statement about ourselves and how we view ourselves. The impression we make when we first walk into a room can be the lasting one and is particularly important at interviews.

So how can we ensure that the message we are sending out is one of confidence and competence?

1   Think positively
2   Look good, feel good
3   Make eye-contact with people – don't look down or away. It transmits confidence and helps listening. (If you find it too uncomfortable to look someone straight in the eye focus your eyes just above the other person's – it will look as if you are looking at them and will help you not to feel embarrassed.)
4   Walk tall
5   Relax your shoulders – don't hunch them or try to make yourself look smaller
6   Take a few deep breaths and let your breath out very slowly. It will calm you down and you will feel your body relaxing
7   Speak calmly but firmly and not too fast. Think of people you know who always seem very confident. Write down what it is about them that gives that air of confidence.

Now think about yourself; do you have any habits or traits that give the impression of a lack of confidence? One thing women often do is to apologise unnecessarily. Think back to the people who appear confident and write down some of the things you can do to appear more like them. It will be difficult at first, but if you practice on one thing at a time you will gradually build up your confidence. The next time you walk into a room full of strangers pick one person who looks friendly and go up and introduce yourself. You may find it helpful to go on an assertiveness training course.

DRAWING UP AN ACTION PLAN

Building confidence is the first step towards getting back to work. But not only back to work. It is the first step in making sure that the job you get is the one you want – the one that will most suit you and help you to get what you want from life.

It is important to recognise why so many women lose their self-confidence when they leave paid employment. You are not the only woman to feel like this. It happens to us all. Knowing this should help you to see that rebuilding your confidence is not impossible. You can get help along the way, from friends and family, from books, by talking to other women like yourself, and by going on courses.

But it can still be a daunting prospect and the best way to start is to plan your course of action. You need to write down what you are going to do and when you are going to do it. Action plans need to be simple and practical. Below is a model of an action plan. Yours will be personal to you, but if you follow the guidelines it will help you to achieve your goals.

Take a sheet of paper. Divide it into seven columns across the page as follows:

Goals ● People and things that will help ● Actions ● People and things that will hinder ● Actions ● Summary of Actions ● Date when achieved

For each goal that you have identified think of everything and everyone that can help you to achieve it. Write down the actions that you can take to build on those things that will help. Now write down everything and everyone that will hinder you and write down the actions that you can take to minimise the hindrances.

Now make a summary of the actions you can take and a date by which you will have taken them. Be realistic and keep your actions simple and achievable. The very process of making an action plan and making a start will help to increase your confidence. You will find that one action, however simple, opens the way to others and that soon you will be well along the path towards your particular goals. Some actions won't be successful, but that is not important. What is more, we normally learn more from our mistakes than from our successes.

The one golden rule is that there is no golden rule. Everyone will have her own priorities and there is no right way. It is important to recognise, too, that simply by starting to take action you will change things and that as a result your goals might change. Action plans are not written in tablets of stone; they need to be reviewed regularly and revised as necessary. But by having a plan of action you will feel a greater sense of direction and control and the problems will become challenges.

Good luck!

FURTHER INFORMATION

USEFUL ADDRESSES

DOMINO CONSULTANCY LTD
56 Charnwood Road, Shepshed, Leicestershire LE12 9NP
Tel: (0509) 505404
PEPPERELL UNIT
The Industrial Society, Robert Hyde House, 48 Bryanston Square, London W1H 7LN
Tel: (071) 262 2401

WOMEN'S ENTERPRISE DEVELOPMENT AGENCY
Aston Science Park, Love Lane, Aston Triangle, Birmingham B7 4BJ
Tel: (021) 359 0178
WOMEN RETURNERS NETWORK
Euston House, 81–103 Euston Street, London NW1 2ET
Tel: (071) 388 3111   Contact: Ruth Michael (Chair)
WORKING MOTHERS ASSOCIATION
77 Holloway Road, London N7 8JZ
Tel: (071) 700 5771

USEFUL BOOKS

- *Returning Without Fears*, Domino Consultancy
- *Superconfidence*, Gael Lindenfield, Thorsons

TWO

EDUCATION &
TRAINING

CATHERINE McCARTHY

Catherine McCarthy is an Education Officer for BBC Education currently working in the Equal Opportunities Unit of the Continuing Education Department.

Her work at the BBC has been mainly with programmes about women, carers, and people's rights and benefits. Catherine has also worked on the BBC's programme for women returners, 'Women Mean Business', and she is currently working on the new series for women, 'Great Expectations'.

Before joining the BBC she worked for SHELTER as a training officer and prior to that she was a school teacher.

INTRODUCTION

There is no single, organised system of education and training in this country which will deliver you just what you want and need. We do not have a system which is centrally planned. Different areas of the country have different policies and therefore the provision of education varies greatly between them. Although this means that our system is more flexible than those of other countries, it also means that it can be hard finding out what is available.

Hundreds of organisations now offer opportunities to learn – from colleges to Government programmes to private companies. Increasingly, colleges are becoming more aware of the sort of support women need in order to learn and they are trying to make courses more accessible to people who, in the past, have not been able to take up educational opportunities. New courses are being set up all the time, especially in the private sector where companies are worried about shortages of skilled workers. However, in the public sector, some courses may be squeezed out owing to lack of money.

For women wanting to return to paid work, now is a relatively good time to get some training or education. You will find that there are many more opportunities available now than ever before. You will have a far wider range of subjects to choose from and the possibility of studying them in more flexible ways.

A large number of courses now exists for adults coming back into education, some specifically for women. For many people these offer a completely different experience of learning from the one they had at school. One of the most important things about these courses is that they help to rebuild confidence by providing a supportive learning environment.

If you do decide to take a course, you may encounter difficulties along the way, perhaps in actually trying to find out what is available, or in fighting your way through the grants system. It might be hard to arrange childcare and cope with new demands on your time and other people's attitudes towards your study. Or you may fear that you will run into financial problems. But going on a course or learning new skills should be a rewarding experience and worth the sacrifices and hard work it involves. It will certainly help you to develop confidence and will ease the transition between home and work.

This chapter, then, is not a directory of courses, but it will give you some signposts as to where to get advice and information about them. It will give some examples of the sort of courses available, both if you are starting from scratch or if you want to update your skills. It also focuses on some of the areas of employment which are likely to be worst hit by shortages of skilled people and looks at refresher and updating courses. Information about the costs of study and where to get advice about grants is also included.

We hope the information in this chapter will be useful to women in a range of different situations and at different stages, from those wanting to return to study for the second time, to those wanting to update skills and return to their previous jobs or professional areas.

DECIDING ON YOUR COURSE

WHERE DO YOU START?

You have been at home looking after your children for a while. You are thinking about going back to paid work and you are considering taking a course or doing some training. Perhaps you don't know where to start, you're not sure what you can do, you feel out of touch and wonder what is available. You might feel like this woman:

> When I decided to return to work, several years ago, I remember thinking to myself 'I just don't know what I can do'. I felt as if I had no skills and nothing to offer. And the worst thing was the really big question – where do I start?

If this sounds like you, don't despair, because information and advice are available, and this chapter will help you to find them. But first you will need to spend some time thinking, planning and working out what you want to do. The following pages will enable you to begin this process by running through the sort of things you will need to think about, and by signposting you to the places you can go to for helpful advice and information.

WHAT DO YOU WANT TO DO?

Your first step is to think carefully about what you want to do. It may have been a long time since you last studied and you now need new skills and qualifications to get the job you want. Alternatively, you may want to update skills which you have not used for a while, develop confidence, get help writing your Curriculum Vitae, or preparing for a job interview. You may decide to retrain and change direction – many women use the return from their break as the opportunity to do something new. Here are some of your options:

- A course which prepares you generally for paid work by helping to build your confidence, or by giving practice with interviews or job search.
- A further education or training qualification, so that you can apply for jobs for which you are not at present qualified.
- A course which helps you to update your skills and knowledge so that you can return to your job or profession.
- A course which enables you to acquire new skills or retrain, so that you can change direction in your career.
- A course which will prepare you to set up your own business (see Chapter 7).

You may feel that you need to talk through your options with somebody. You could talk to your family and friends, and you could contact one of the services listed in this chapter.

WHAT IF YOU DON'T
KNOW WHAT YOU WANT TO DO?

How do you decide what to do? For many people this is the hardest part. As one woman said:

> I feel overwhelmed by the possibilities, and I just don't know where to start. I need help defining what it is I want to do, and with recognising my strengths.

It can be difficult working out what you want to do, and far from easy finding out what sort of courses are available to help you to do it. You will need to think about the skills and abilities you have and the things that you enjoy doing (see Chapter 1). Having a clearer idea of your skills should help you to narrow down the kind of area that you would like to study and work in.

If possible you should try and find someone who can advise you, to whom you can talk openly about the skills that you have, and who can advise you on possible courses and careers. Whether there is someone near at hand who can do this depends on where you live. If you would like this kind of help, contact your Educational Guidance Service or Careers Office (see pages 45–49 for more details).

WHEN YOU KNOW WHAT TO DO – WHAT NEXT?

Once you have some idea about what you want to do, you will need to:

- Find out what courses are available and whether you have the qualifications to do them. However, many courses don't require any prior qualifications.
- Find out if the qualifications they offer will lead to a job.
- Find out if there are going to be job vacancies available once you have done the course.
- Check all the practical details – how long the course will last, how many hours of study are involved both at college and at home, the cost and whether grants are available, whether childcare is provided, and how far you will have to travel.

You may need help and advice with these things, so contact one of the agencies below. Don't be put off if you don't get the answers you want first time around – you might have to keep trying.

FINDING OUT ABOUT COURSES

There is a variety of help available ranging from computer-based information to one-to-one counselling.

Services providing advice and information	Services providing information only
Educational Guidance Service	Library
Careers Office	Newspapers
Job Centre	Women Returners' Directory
Citizens Advice Bureau	
Colleges	
Careers for Women	
Computer-based Advice	**Computer-based Information**
The Women Returners' Project	Training Access Points

The following section of this chapter gives more information about each of these services, what they can offer, and how you can contact them.

SERVICES PROVIDING ADVICE AND INFORMATION

EDUCATIONAL GUIDANCE SERVICE

This service is available in many parts of the UK, but not all. It comes under different names such as Education Shop, Learning Links or Educational Advice. If there isn't a service in your area, you will be able to go to that of a neighbouring area. Educational Guidance is a free local service aimed particularly at adults. Women returners are one of their main client groups. According to one adviser from Southwark Education and Training Shop,

> The majority of enquirers who come to us are people with few or no previous qualifications, who have been out of education for some time. Building confidence for such enquirers can be as essential as providing information on what opportunities are available. Many enquirers, especially women, may make an initial enquiry into one area of education, but after coming to talk to us decide to take quite a different course in their careers.

Every service is different but they all provide advisers who will sit down with you, and help you work through your various choices and options. Some operate on a 'drop-in' basis, others will ask you to make an appointment and come back at a later date. They provide information, advice and counselling on education, training and work opportunities in your area from basic education to post-graduate level. Most have leaflets, guides and a database of information on local courses. They are there to help you decide what you want to do and to give you the information you need to follow your choice through.

> Anwara went to see an adviser at her local Educational Guidance Service. She had no previous qualifications and was returning to education after bringing up her children and doing voluntary work. She was interested in teaching or social work. The adviser explained about Fresh Start and Access courses. During the conversation, it became clear that Anwara had always had a secret ambition to get a degree. She has now

decided to apply for an Access course which leads to a four-year degree course in Social Studies.
                              Southwark Education and Training Shop

Ask at your local library, Job Centre or Careers Office for details of your local Educational Guidance Service.

CAREERS OFFICE

While the careers service was set up to advise school leavers, in some areas it offers advice to adults too. If it does it is likely that it will provide a service similar to Educational Guidance, described above. You will be able to make an appointment and talk to an adviser who will help you work through your various options. It should have a collection of information and reference books about courses and jobs, covering what is available in your area and further afield. You should be able to track down your local careers service by looking in the telephone directory under Career Guidance Services, or by asking at your local library.

JOB CENTRE

Your local Job Centre will be able to give you information about the Government Training Scheme – Employment Training, or Job Training in Northern Ireland (for more details see page 66). It should also be able to tell you about other sorts of training and retraining programmes available in your area. Job Centres can advise on skills shortages in your area (and other areas if you are thinking of moving). The address will be in your local telephone directory, or available at your library.

CITIZENS ADVICE BUREAU (CAB)

Your local CAB might well be able to help you locate courses in your area. Details of your local office should be in the telephone directory or at the library.

COLLEGES

Once you have decided you are interested in a particular course, telephone the college and ask them to send you course details. It is also worth asking to see someone from the department running the course. It's usual for people in Education – teachers, tutors, heads of department – to talk to prospective students to help them find out if a course is suitable. Some colleges have a member of staff responsible for student guidance – ask at your college to find out if there is a person who does this. Here is some information about what the various colleges have to offer. There are overlaps between what they provide but this is a general guide:

● *Adult Education Centres* – These offer evening classes and day classes of every kind, from flower arranging to A-level Spanish, including Return to Study and Women Returners' Courses.
● *Colleges of Further Education* – These colleges offer general educational courses and vocational training below degree level.
● *Polytechnics* – These mainly offer degree courses with a vocational bias, plus some courses below degree level: full, part-time and short courses.
● *Universities* – These mainly offer degree and postgraduate courses.

CAREERS FOR WOMEN

Careers for Women is an educational charity which advises on education, training and career opportunities for women returners, or those already at work who wish to change direction. It provides career advice interviews which last about one hour and cost £57.50 at the time of publication. Make an appointment first.

Although based in London, they do provide a national service, and answer queries and give interviews to women all over the country. If you want advice locally, they will be able to refer you to a named person, or they will travel out of London to meet a minimum of three women – but you will have to pay their fare! They also provide a postal information service answering specific questions about careers (£5.75). One-day workshops are also run called A Fresh Look which provide information and guidance on career planning (£37.00). Their address and telephone number are at the end of this chapter.

THE WOMEN RETURNERS' PROJECT

The Women Returners' Project is a computer-based career guidance system for women returners, aiming to help you find out what your interests are and what you want to do. The system is designed to be friendly and easy to use. It will ask you questions about your interests, experience and aspirations and suggest possible career options. You will be able to print out details of any career which you are interested in and where to get further local information. It should be found in some Careers Offices and Colleges of Further Education. The system is being linked to Training Access Points (see page 51) where possible, to provide information on local training opportunities. (For further details about the Women Returners' Project see the address list at the end of this chapter.)

SERVICES PROVIDING INFORMATION ONLY

LIBRARY

Your library is a good place to look for information. Although libraries cannot make someone available to go through books and leaflets with you, they do have an information desk so you can ask for the sort of things you are looking for. Most libraries have books on a range of different careers, professions and jobs. Look in the reference section for these and for courses run at Polytechnics, Universities, Adult Education Institutes and Colleges of Further Education.

NEWSPAPERS

Some newspapers advertise courses for women returners, so it's always worth keeping an eye out in the press. Your local library is likely to have copies of all local and national papers.

WOMEN RETURNERS' DIRECTORY

RETURNING TO WORK:
A DIRECTORY OF EDUCATION AND TRAINING FOR WOMEN

The Women Returners' Network have compiled a directory listing 1400 courses for women returners in the UK, with details of how to apply, entry requirements, costs, qualifications and childcare facilities. The directory costs £9.95 and can be bought from most major bookshops. But it would be worth checking to see if your library has a copy before going out and buying your own.

TRAINING ACCESS POINTS (TAPs)

TAP is a computerised system set up to provide information about local full- and part-time education and training opportunities, covering all sorts of providers, such as colleges, private organisations, voluntary bodies, chambers of commerce and more. Currently, TAPs are available in thirty areas in the country. Mobile TAPs can be found in libraries, Job Centres and some supermarkets, but few are staffed. (For further details see the address list at the end of this chapter.)

WILL A COURSE LEAD TO A JOB?

Before committing yourself to a course, it's worth finding out about the job situation in your particular area. You will need to know where the job openings are likely to be, at what level and whether the course you want to do is likely to increase your chances of getting a job.

The skills shortages will be affecting all areas of employment over the next decade, so there will be a demand for skilled workers, but these shortages will vary across the country. As a direct response to this situation, the Government is in the process of establishing The Training and Enterprise Councils, TECs, in England and Wales (or Local Enterprise Councils, LECs, in Scotland). TECs will control much of the funding for vocational training (ie, training for work), for young people and adults. They are being set up as a response to the very low level of training in the UK, and they will be encouraging employers to fund training which is specifically linked to overcoming skills shortages in local areas. Therefore, they will be enabling people to become trained for jobs where there are vacancies.

At the moment it is unclear how all TECs and LECs will work, as only a few have been set up. But it does seem likely that there will be more training available which is directly linked to work. To find out more about the TECs and the skills shortages, contact your Job Centre or Careers Office.

Colleges and employers are increasingly working together to recruit and train people for identified local skills shortages. This is called customised training. Recruitment is undertaken jointly; the training is usually provided by the College and work placement by the employer. The advantage of this kind of course is that it is linked to specific job vacancies, and offers employment on successful completion of the course.

Watch out in the local press for details of this kind of training or ask at your local college to find out whether they run any courses linked to local employers. Your local Careers Service or Job Centre should also have information.

There are other ways of finding out if a course will lead to a job. You could ask the course tutor how many past students have got jobs and how long it took. You could check the local papers for job vacancies over several weeks. You could even try phoning the Personnel Department of companies or organisations and asking what sort of vacancies are available.

CHECKING PRACTICAL DETAILS

One reason why it can be hard to find out about courses is that there are so many different kinds on offer: part-time, full-time, college based, open learning. They might be run in the evenings only, or in the summer holidays, or follow the college term. While some courses are run at times that might be more or less impossible for you, such as in the summer holidays, others have been organised with the needs of mothers with young children in mind. One good example is at the University of Ulster, where a new course, The Certificate in Information Technology Studies, was designed and made available for women in Northern Ireland. When the course was being set up careful attention was paid to:

- Providing free creche facilities and financial assistance for travel costs.
- Arranging the timetable to fit in with school hours, i.e. 10am–3pm, with Friday study optional.
- Confidence building, which included giving students help with keyboard skills, study skills, and communication skills.
- Giving students the option of ongoing guidance and counselling throughout the course.
- Ensuring that no prior qualifications were needed to get on to the course.
- Ensuring that the course was taught by women, thereby providing good role models for the students.

Not all courses are as well designed as this one, but many offer some of the above features.

Once you have decided on a possible course, you will need to check a number of practical details to make sure that the course is suitable for you There are some practical details that you may need to check. Use the following questions as a checklist.

- How many weeks will the course last?
- What are the exact dates?
- What are the times and days I will need to be in college?
- How do I apply?
- What entry qualifications do I need?
- Is there any fee? Will there be any extra expenses?
- Are there any grants available?
- How is the course assessed?
- Are students given help with learning to study?
- Is there a creche? Does the creche have any places? Does it charge a fee?

- If I need extra help with English Language, what classes are there?
- What would my job prospects be after taking the course?

THE COURSES THEMSELVES

There are many different types of learning opportunities available, ranging from short, confidence-booster courses to academic qualifications to skills training. Many of these could provide you with new challenges and the opportunity to do something for yourself.

This section covers courses which could help you make a new start and ultimately lead you in a new and perhaps different direction in your career. It also covers courses which could help you update existing or rusty skills and return to your particular field of paid work.

MAKING A NEW START

For many adults, taking a course has been a major turning point in their lives – perhaps because it has been the springboard into paid work or more education, or because it has helped them develop confidence and new belief in themselves and their abilities.

Returning to Education is now far more possible, largely because there has been a huge growth of new courses specially designed to encourage adults back into the education system. Many people left school without fulfilling their full potential, and these courses enable them to have a second chance. Some are for women returners, others are for men and women, but are often largely taken up by women. As well as these, there are lots of classes for adults where you can work towards the 'traditional' qualifications like GCSEs.

This section covers the range of adult learning opportunities available including Second Chance courses (discussion groups, returner courses, Access and Open Learning courses), general education courses, and training for work. What these courses have in common is that you can start any of them from scratch, and they could provide you with a vital stepping stone to paid work and to taking a new direction in your life.

SECOND CHANCE COURSES

INFORMAL DISCUSSION GROUPS

Jan is a single parent, with little previous work experience and no formal qualifications. She spent several years at home looking after her two children. By chance, she found out about a discussion group for women taking place at her local school. She was feeling so isolated that she plucked up the courage to go along. At the group she found out about a New Opportunities for Women course being run at her local college. While she was doing this course, she heard about a Women into Technology course, again being run at her local college. She had always been interested in this area, and by this time she was feeling confident enough to tackle something new. So she decided to do the course. She is now teaching on the course, and taking a teacher training qualification at her local Teacher Training College.

For some women, like Jan, the path through education starts quite informally, perhaps at a coffee morning run at a local school or a parent/discussion group run by a local community centre. These groups are being set up all the time, and they are an important way of opening up opportunities for women and giving them the chance to do something for themselves away from the home. Two women from a discussion group, based at a school in Birmingham, said:

I came here first for the children, because it gives me a break from the housework.

It's been good to have somewhere to go, to get new ideas and meet new people.

Their discussion group meets every week from 9.15 am to 11.15 am, at their children's school. The group consists of eight women and they decide with the group tutor the areas they want to cover and what they feel is relevant to their lives. They have talked about topics such as relationships, children, relaxation, self-defence, future careers, allotments and books. They have visited local colleges, and are considering the possibility of doing a GCSE together. One woman, who later went on to do a New Opportunities for Women course, said of the group:

It was a springboard for me at that time, and I've gone from strength to strength.

Many women go on from this type of group to other things, such as a New Opportunities for Women course, or a Return to Work or Study course.

To find out if a group like this exists in your area ask at your school, community centre, library, health centre or playgroup or look out for posters or leaflets on noticeboards. If one doesn't exist perhaps you could set one up. You could gather a group of women together, approach your Local Adult Education Department and ask them to provide a group tutor.

RETURNER COURSES

These courses are specially for adults (some are women only) who want to come back into education or prepare to return to paid work. They come under a variety of different names, such as:

Return to Study
Return to Learn
Return to Work
New Opportunities for Women (NOW)
New Start
Fresh Start
New Directions
Second Chance to Learn
New Horizons
Access Courses

While these courses vary in length, price and subject matter, they *all* have certain features in common. They:

● don't require formal qualifications.
● provide a supportive environment.
● aim to rebuild confidence.
● help you work out what you want to do next.
● are run at appropriate and flexible times.
● are focused around your needs – courses are adjusted to respond to students' needs.
● are designed so that you can keep your career options open.

Often these courses are specially designed with the needs of women and people from ethnic minorities in mind. Some are structured to help people who may have special needs due to disability, age, race or sex.

Although they are all for adults coming back into education, they are not all at the same level. There are several levels ranging from basic communication skills courses to Access courses (courses which prepare you for degree level – see next section). Some will help you take stock of your own situation and look at the options available to you in work and study, while others will give you skills to help you return to paid work.

As well as general courses there are many which offer subjects or skills such as Women and New Technology, or Maths Fresh Start for Women. Some include basic maths or English, and some are for people whose first language is not English. Many particularly welcome black women. Because there is such a variety, it's important that you find the course that's right for you, so shop around and get advice from your Educational Guidance or Careers Service.

These courses can be immensely useful to women who are thinking about returning to paid work, as they will give you the opportunity to rethink your life with other people who are likely to be in exactly the same position. Ann did a New Opportunities for Women course at Strathclyde University which ran for four weeks, two days a week. The course took account of family commitments by starting at 10 am and finishing at 3 pm. She said:

> At the beginning of the course we were nervous, we were unsure of each other although it was quite clear we were all women in the same situation who had either left work to bring up children or gone abroad for various reasons.

The course looked at work, study and self-employment options and spent time helping women develop their Curriculum Vitae and interview techniques.

These courses are run at Adult Education Centres, F.E. Colleges, a few Polytechnics and Universities and by the

Workers Education Association (WEA). They are not always free – but, wherever possible, help is given if you are unable to cover the costs. Even so, it can be difficult, and many women find the cost a problem. One student on a Return to Learn Course said:

> I decided to return to study after a break of nearly ten years. This course is really helping me and I've now decided I want to go on to do an Access to Social Work course. I am a single parent, and it's often very difficult for me to carry on, mainly because of the money, but I'm determined to build a better future for myself and my daughter and that's what makes me carry on.

ACCESS COURSES
Many colleges now run Access courses which are designed to give students without qualifications a route into University, Polytechnic or Institutes of Higher Education. They provide a recognised alternative to A-levels and Highers.

You will not need any formal qualifications to do an Access course, but your competence in English and Maths may have to be assessed. These courses normally take one year of full-time study or two years of part-time, and you may be able to get a grant from your Local Education Authority. Many Colleges run courses which are under 21 hours per week – this is important if you are receiving benefits (see page 85).

Some Access courses are linked to a particular degree course so that if you are successful on the Access course you will get an automatic place on the degree course. Not all Access courses give you a guaranteed place though, but many Universities, Polytechnics and Institutes of Higher Education will look favourably on the course when you apply. It's worth checking very carefully where your course will lead you before making a decision.

Access courses aim to give a foundation in a range of skills and understanding. While most provide an introduction to arts, humanities or social sciences, there are now increasing numbers of science, engineering and health studies courses. Some are directly linked to taking further qualifications in a particular professional area, such as Access to Law, Access to Nursing, Access to Social Work or Community and Youth Work, Access to Information/Technology/Engineering for Women, Access to Teaching.

Access courses can be an important way back into the system for women who have been at home for a while. They can help to move you on to other things.

> Linda became interested in studying again when she moved from Newcastle to London and started living in a block of flats which was full of students. She said that she began to realise 'how little I knew' and that she couldn't face the prospect of doing clerical work all her life. She went along to her Educational Guidance Service with no idea of what she wanted to do or where to start. They helped her find a one-year, full-time, Access course in Social Science which had a guaranteed place at a Polytechnic. She said, 'the course was brilliant, we were all in the same boat – our main problem was confidence'. Later she went on to the three-year degree course, which she found quite different from her Access course. She felt that she really struggled, mainly because there was less readily available support. Now she has completed her degree and is planning to take another course so that she can eventually become a clinical psychologist.

Whether or not there is a suitable Access course near you depends very much on where you live. There are growing numbers of these courses available in Scotland, Northern

Ireland and Wales. For information about Access courses, contact your local Educational Guidance Service, Careers Service or College of Further Education.

RESIDENTIAL STUDY

There are seven long-term residential colleges in England and Wales. They offer full-time courses which provide a context for people to combine serious full-time study with counselling and guidance about a range of opportunities including higher education, vocational training and employment. The choice of progression routes is determined by the student. Residential study is possible for women with children who are able to make childcare arrangements.

Hillcroft College in Surrey is the only one of these residential colleges which is for women. It runs one- and two-year courses for women over the age of 21 years who have no formal qualifications. Students on full-time courses receive a mandatory grant. All courses help to prepare women for further study (such as degree courses) or to return to work. For further details, contact the college (the address is at the end of this chapter).

Mandy is a first-year day-student at Hillcroft College. She has a five-year-old daughter. This year she has studied a range of subjects including social history and sociology. Next year she hopes to study psychology and drama.

Above all, the experience at Hillcroft has helped me develop confidence and a positive attitude about myself. This is to do with Hillcroft's setting, the non-competitive environment, the tutors, who are encouraging and supportive and the fact that every person's experience is valued.

OPEN AND FLEXIBLE LEARNING

You may prefer working from materials – books, study packs and cassettes – in your own time to studying with other students in college. If so, you could take an Open College or Open University Course. Open learning facilities are also becoming more available at Colleges of Further Education, some Polytechnics, Universities, Adult Education Centres, correspondence colleges and the Open College of the Arts. While you may spend some time in a discussion group with a tutor, for much of the time you will be working on your own.

This method of study could be particularly useful if you live a long way away from a college, although you will be working on your own a great deal and you may find it hard to motivate yourself.

THE OPEN COLLEGE

The Open College is linked to broadcasting and offers a number of different Open Learning courses. Their emphasis is on retraining and updating skills for work. Currently, they are running two courses specifically for women returners, Women – the Way Ahead, and Return to Nursing (see page 78). They also run a variety of other courses which may be of interest.

Women – The Way Ahead, has been designed to help women of all ages make the most of new opportunities on offer. It will help you to recognise your strengths and weaknesses, develop yourself and take constructive steps towards your chosen career. The course is particularly suitable for women who are returning to paid work after having a family and are looking for a new direction or needing advice on coping with demands of home and work. Course materials include a workbook, textbook, video and audio tape.

This course takes approximately 30 hours study time, and can lead to a SCOTVEC National Certificate in Job Seeking

Skills. Tutorial support is available from most recommended centres. The course costs £30. Details are available from The Open College. (Their address is at the end of this chapter.)

THE OPEN UNIVERSITY

The Open University provides a wide range of educational opportunities for people who want to study in their own home and in their own time. It is unique in that it caters for mature students and you do not need qualifications to get on to a course. As well as offering degree and higher degree (MSc or MA) courses, the Open University also offers non-degree courses. Two of these are specifically for women, Women into Management, and Women into Technology. For further details of all courses contact The Open University (see the end of the chapter for address).

Courses vary in price; there may be fee concessions from the Open University for people who are unemployed, or your Local Education Authority may help with the cost of Summer School. Here's how one woman managed to work and study.

Ursula taught in a Primary School for several years before having ten years away from paid work to bring up her four children. She then went back to teaching full time. It was only when all her children had gone to University and got degrees that she felt that this was something she had missed out on. She said 'I needed something stimulating and interesting; something for me, away from my job and family'. She spent seven years working for an Open University degree in humanities as well as working full-time as Head of an Infants School. She said, 'The course consisted of working through course material which the Open University sent, writing assignments, attending three week-long Summer Schools, going to local tutorials and *following the Open University Radio and Television programmes. I worked in the evenings, at weekends and during the holidays. It was hard work but worth it, because it was immensely personally fulfilling'.*

OPEN COLLEGE NETWORKS

As well as Open College and Open University courses you may find that your local Adult Education Service is part of an Open College Network. This is quite different from the Open College already mentioned above. Open College Networks exist in a growing number of areas, and they enable people to accumulate credits for a whole range of educational courses which hitherto have not led to formal qualifications. If you are interested in building up credits in this way, and then using them to progress to more formal qualifications, find out if there is an Open College Network operating in your area. An Open College Network could help you design a learning package specific to your own individual needs.

GENERAL EDUCATION COURSES

As well as the courses already mentioned in this chapter, which are specifically designed to give adults alternatives to traditional qualifications, it is worth considering the range of general courses like GCSEs, A-levels or Highers, which could improve your chances of getting a job. It is not too late to get these qualifications, and there are lots of classes specially for adults. Some jobs ask for a certain level of academic qualification – such as 5 GCSEs or a degree. While these courses won't actually train you for a job or even prepare you in terms of subject matter, they do indicate to employers that you have reached a certain standard. So, if you are interested in a particular job, find out if certain qualifications are necessary. You may be interested in:

1 Adult or Community Education Classes

While some of these classes are for leisure or hobbies and do not lead to a formal qualification, they can be a good first step on the road to a higher qualification such as a GCSE. They can also give you a chance to try out a new interest which may then develop into a job. Many Colleges are now developing 'Accreditation Systems' so that you can get a certificate for the study you've completed.

2 Adult Basic Education

To help you catch up with reading, writing or maths. This can be useful for people who need to improve their basic skills or for people whose first language is not English. These classes could lead you on to further study and increase your confidence.

3 Traditional Qualifications

Working for qualifications like GCSE, A-levels, Highers.

4 Higher Education

Degree courses and Postgraduate study at Universities or Polytechnics. Some Polytechnics and the Open University offer associate student schemes on many of their courses. This means that you will be able to study single units of courses and you don't have to enrol to do the whole course. You will be able to build up these single units or 'credits', and accumulate them towards getting a degree or whatever the final qualification may be. You will be able to pace your study as you can take units over a period of time and at different colleges. For more details contact your Polytechnic or the Open University.

There is one 'women only' University College in Cambridge, called Lucy Cavendish, for women over the age of 25 who want to study for degrees. It is important because you do not have to have A-level qualifications to get in – but you will be asked to sit an entrance exam. For more details contact the college (see address list for details).

Visit your local library or Educational Guidance Service for more information about general educational courses.

TRAINING FOR WORK

EMPLOYMENT TRAINING

The Government Programme, Employment Training, or Job Training in Northern Ireland, is for people over 18 and under 60, mainly those who have been registered unemployed for six months or more. It offers a range of training to give you skills to help you return to work or become self-employed. The range is broad, from basic numeracy and literacy to higher level skills, with the emphasis on training for vocational qualifications for all types of jobs. ET lasts up to twelve months and starts with an initial period of guidance, then a period of practical training with an employer, combined with time spent at a college or training centre. When the TECs are fully set up, they will develop ET so that unemployed people are trained for local jobs.

Women returners can be admitted to ET without being registered unemployed if they have been away from employment for at least two years for domestic reasons, e.g. raising a family or caring for elderly relatives. They have, however, a secondary priority of access to ET. Part-time training is available for women returners and for lone parents and people with disabilities. Lone parents may also receive support with the cost of childcare. All ET trainees receive a weekly allowance. For more details about ET, contact your Job Centre.

PROFESSIONAL UPDATING COURSES

These courses were started at Hatfield Polytechnic. They are now being run at five different centres:

- Humberside Polytechnic
- Manchester Polytechnic
- Nottingham Polytechnic
- Exeter University
- Strathclyde University

These nine-week courses are for women with degrees or professional qualifications who are contemplating returning to paid work. You will be eligible if you practised your profession for two years before taking a break.

They aim to help you prepare to re-enter employment and take up your career with confidence. You will also be updated on what has been happening in your field and what will be expected of you in current practice. The courses pro-

vide practical help with job search and applications. Courses are free and students have a small allowance of £10.00 per week as well as help with travel expenses and childcare.

Women on these courses come from a range of professions such as social work, personnel, town planning, account-ancy, business, administration, and law. The course involves a work placement of one day per week plus one whole week. This gives the opportunity for you to 'test out' how work will feel. Three days a week are spent at the Uni-versity or College looking at how to prepare a CV, interview techniques, assertiveness, new legislation and personal finance. At Humberside, 10 out of 12 students have gone back to work at the same level or higher. Here is how one woman from the Exeter course found a job:

> Susan is a Chartered Accountant. She trained and worked in this field for several years before taking seven years out to bring up three children. She decided to return to work because her family were growing up and there was less to do at home. She is the local organiser of the National Women's Register and it was through this that she found out about the Professional Updating Course at Exeter University. She said the best thing about the course was the work placement, which gave her the chance to get back in. She has been lucky enough to be offered a job as a Senior Accountant by the firm she had her placement with, and she has negotiated part-time work with the school holidays off! She says 'The course really helped and gave me the confidence and contacts to go back to work'.

For further information, contact your Job Centre or Educa-tional Guidance Service. Other updating courses are being set up in specific professional areas (see Updating your skills on the next page).

UPDATING YOUR SKILLS

Over the next ten years it is likely that all sectors of our economy will face shortages of skilled workers. These shortages will vary greatly in different areas of the country.

In some professions, such as teaching, nursing and information technology, and in some parts of the country, the shortages are already acute so that employers and professional bodies have had to develop re-training or refresher courses to try to attract workers back. Other areas where skills shortages have already been reported are in computing, accountancy, engineering, manual trades (such as carpentry and welding), clerical work, sales and finance.

Other fields, such as journalism, arts and media, have not yet been affected by the skills shortages. This is likely to be because these jobs have always been very popular and there is still fierce competition for them. Therefore, within these professions, there is very little training specifically for women who wish to return.

Overall, the provision of updating training for women returning to their profession is limited and patchy, and it is hard to find out what is available. In many cases, women return to their jobs after taking statutory maternity leave or a longer career break with no training at all. Or they leave their paid jobs for a longer time and when they decide to return it's a case of applying for jobs and battling it out with everyone else.

The best advice is, if you have already trained in a particular area and would like to know what opportunities are available to enable you to get back, contact your relevant Professional Body or National Training Organisations (formerly many of these were Industrial Training Boards).

The following section gives some examples of the sort of courses which are available for women wanting to return to their professions, and lists the organisations, support groups and networks which you can go to for more information and advice. All addresses are at the back of the chapter.

INFORMATION TECHNOLOGY AND OFFICE SKILLS

Information Technology and office skills are areas where severe skills shortages are predicted over the next few years. In 1988, the National Curriculum Council Report 'The Information Technology Skills Crisis: the way ahead', predicted a need for a 40 per cent increase in the number of Information Technology trainees. It estimated that 100 000 people were needed to train in Information Technology at a professional level by 1993. The report also said that the gap must be met by better use of women IT staff who are currently a falling proportion of the industry's workforce.

Information Technology is a phrase used to encompass the management and communication of information, using computerised systems. It involves working on a computer using, for example, a word processor or database. Now many jobs require a knowledge of and expertise with computers, and because technology is changing all the time this causes problems for women returners. If you had computer skills before taking a break, you will probably need to update your skills. If you had secretarial skills, you will probably need to learn about computers. As one woman said:

> It would have been quite impossible for me to go back into computing without retraining and really, until now, retraining has not been available at the sort of level I wanted.

COMPUTING
Courses are available at Further Education and Higher Education Colleges in different areas of computing, such as pro-

gramming or word processing. There are also a number of private organisations providing training – contact the National Computing Centre for details. There are a few courses specifically for returners, like the one Jane did.

Jane was a computer analyst before having 10 years away from paid work to look after her children. When she first considered returning, she said: 'I thought it was going to be impossible – computing has changed so much over the last 15 years'. But, she found a 12-week refresher course at her local university, specifically for women who were previously trained to her level. The course involved a work placement at a local company. Jane said: 'We've all gone back to the classroom to re-learn the skills we once had. We were all reasonably highly skilled before we left computing. It's actually fun to go back to learn something'.

When she finishes the course, Jane hopes to get a part-time job with a local company at a similar level to the job she had before.

Courses like the one Jane did are few and far between, but it is likely that they will increase. If you are interested in this sort of training, find out if it is run in your area. Your Educational Guidance or Careers Service should be able to help. But do check to make sure that local employers offer work placements or sponsorship for people on the course. It could be very frustrating to complete a Returner course, only to find that there are no jobs available locally.

You may want to do your training in a women-only group. There are a number of Women's Training Centres in the UK which offer courses in computing. They are for women who are unemployed, over the age of 25 and living in the local area. Women returners are one of the groups for which they cater specifically.

Women's Training Centres offer a range of courses, some involving work experience. Many offer technology courses such as computer programming and electronics, which are full-time for one year. The courses are free and you will be given a training allowance, travel expenses and childcare costs. These courses will prepare you for either a higher level course such as an HND or degree, or for work in the area which you've been trained for. For more details contact: The Women's Training Network (see address list).

SECRETARIAL UPDATING

There is likely to be an increased demand for people with secretarial skills in the 1990s – particularly for people who also have computing and word processing skills. If you were originally trained for secretarial work, you may need to update your skills by learning about computing and word processing.

There are a number of places offering courses. You may find that your local Adult Education Centre or College runs courses. These could range from a short word processing course to a two-year full-time course in Business Information Technology. Length, price and content will vary and some will lead to qualifications, but all should help you update skills, build confidence and bring you up-to-date with the latest technology.

In Scotland, Colleges of Further Education run full-time and part-time courses leading to SCOTVEC Certificates and Diplomas. Some run refresher courses, but women returners are welcome on other courses too. Bursaries may be available for full-time study.

Cath decided to take an HND in computer studies at her local Polytechnic to build on her administrative and secretarial skills.

> The three-year course involved one day a week study at the Polytechnic from 9.00 am–9.00 pm. As well as this, a further twelve hours study was expected, which Cath did when her four children had gone to bed. She said, 'the course was in many ways a hard slog; I got no grant and the books were very expensive. But it was interesting, it gave me a feeling for computers, a new social life and the confidence to start applying for jobs'. She now works part-time at a doctors' surgery setting up a computer system.

There are also some private agencies which may be able to help. Some of the large employment agencies, such as Brook Street Bureau, offer the chance to update secretarial skills. Brook Street offers free word processing training at local offices or their training school. Most Brook Street branches have a 'Career come-back' counsellor, who can advise you on how to return to paid work. There is a central telephone number for enquiries (see end of chapter).

Pitmans also offers a range of training from short courses in typing, word processing and shorthand, to longer courses in Business Administration. They are run at different levels and prices vary from approximately £80–£400. For more details contact Pitmans – their telephone number will be in the Yellow Pages under Pitmans Business Training.

BANKING

The major high street banks were the first to offer Career Break, or Return to Work schemes largely because they were worried about the skills shortages and wanted to retain their staff. These schemes vary from bank to bank but most will involve a career break for either parent of between two and five years after the birth of a baby. A career break usually involves a member of staff returning at regular intervals for updating training and/or work experience. The provision at other banks, such as the merchant banks, is more ad hoc.

At Lloyds Bank, the Career Break scheme involves returning for a period of two weeks per year, during the break. The scheme is open to men and women at all grades. One woman on this scheme said:

> It's really good, not only for your own self-esteem and confidence but also for keeping up to date.

But not everyone's experience is like this, and it is sometimes hard for women at more senior levels.

> Gillian worked at a bank as an Assistant Research Manager before taking a statutory maternity break. She returned to find that her department had been drastically cut and her job did not exist. She was offered another job in a different department, at the same grade, but she said, 'It just wasn't the right time to take on something so new, it was too much. I just couldn't work the long hours that were expected of me and cope with looking after a new baby'. After struggling for twelve weeks, she decided to take a longer career break of five years. Ideally, she would like to work part-time, but she will have to drop a grade to do this. As she says, 'It's almost impossible to work part-time at management level. There seems to be such resistance to it'.

If you previously worked at a bank and would like to return but you are not part of a career break scheme, you should contact the Personnel Director at the bank you would like to work for. They may well be interested in recruiting you.

MANUAL TRADES

Currently women make up less than one per cent of the workforce in manual trades. But things are changing and more women are entering craft-trades, such as carpentry and joinery, painting and decorating, plumbing, plastering and bricklaying. There are likely to be more jobs available in this field and employers are going to have to start changing their attitude towards employing women.

Courses can be found at Further Education Colleges, Adult Education Centres and Women's Training Workshops (for women who prefer to train in women-only groups). You should be able to find either a short 'taster' or a more specialist course. These courses are a good way of getting your feet wet and testing out a new area. They will give you a good basis to go on to get further qualifications, such as City and Guilds or Business and Technician Education Council Award (BTEC) or SCOTVEC Certificates. Working in this area may have benefits, such as the opportunity to be self-employed or a good hourly rate of pay.

Contact Women and Manual Trades for advice and information about training courses in this area. They produce a manual costing £2.50 which lists the majority of courses in England.

INDUSTRIAL MANAGEMENT

Women have always faced difficulties getting jobs at senior levels within industry. There is now a severe shortage of highly qualified technology managers in the manufacturing industry and a lack of women in this sector. Women returners face a particularly bleak situation – they are often blocked from returning at a high level and made to feel incompetent because they have taken a break to bring up a family. But things are beginning to change. There are now two centres running Women Into Industry courses.

The University of Bradford runs an 18-month Women Into Industry course, which is a pilot project for women engineers, scientists and technologists returning to manufacturing management. The final six months of this period is spent on a placement in industry.

This course is for women who worked in industry before having a career break or those who want to change direction in their career. It aims to get women with technical backgrounds into management. So, you must have a degree in science, maths, engineering or computing and preferably two years' previous work experience in industry. The course is free but *places are limited*. During the placement you will be paid half a normal salary. On successful completion of the course, women will obtain an MSc in Manufacturing Management.

Cranfield Institute of Technology (Bedford) also runs a similar course, lasting one year. For more details contact the colleges direct.

ENGINEERING

One of the main shortages so far reported is for professional engineers. Engineering courses are now widely available at Further Education, Higher Education and private colleges. There are also a few 'conversion' courses for people (particularly women) looking for a change of direction. They are geared towards people with an Arts/Humanities, educational or non-technical working background, who want to go into the engineering profession. Courses are run at several Universities and Polytechnics. For more details about courses run nationwide contact The University of Liverpool (details are at the end of this chapter).

The Engineering Council is very keen to attract women into engineering and can advise on career breaks for Chartered and Technical Engineers. The Council initiated the Women into Science and Engineering campaign (WISE) which produces a useful booklet covering courses, awards, visits and other initiatives designed to encourage girls and women to consider careers in this area.

The Electrical Engineering Department of the University of Bradford is running a course specifically for women returners. Contact the University for more details.

TEACHING

It is clear that the teaching profession is facing severe short-ages in some subjects and in certain areas of the country. A number of teachers are being recruited from Denmark, Germany and other countries to fill the gaps. Some Local Education Authorities operate 'updating' or 'keeping-in-touch' schemes. Some run Back to the Classroom or Refresher courses for teachers who have taken a break from teaching. For some women, these courses help restore confidence and give them a new sense of direction. As one teacher found out:

> *The Refresher course has helped me decide what direction I want to go in when I return to teaching. The school visits and the course sessions were really valuable and I hope to work with children with learning difficulties when I get back.*

But not everyone's experience is the same. Some women find things are different when they return and they decide to change careers altogether.

> *Cathy came back to full-time teaching as a supply teacher after a ten-year break. She did a Refresher course, but still found it hard to cope in the classroom. She said, 'so much had changed – teaching methods,*

the curriculum and methods of assessment'. She now works part-time and has decided to leave teaching in the near future.

If you do decide to do a course, check that vacancies exist in your subject area and at your level. For details of Refresher courses contact your Local Education Authority. TASC, the Teaching As A Career unit of the Department of Education and Science, holds some information about training openings and can steer you towards the right people to contact in your area. The main Teacher Unions also try to monitor updating opportunities.

NURSING

Nursing is clearly an area where recruitment needs are extremely high. Recruitment policy within the nursing profession is also going to have to change radically if the NHS is going to be kept viable in the 1990s. Several regional health authorities operate 'pools' for nurses who want occasional work, and some run Back to Nursing courses. These aim to ease nurses back into the profession and rebuild confidence.

Helen took a twenty-week Returners' course so that she could resume her career in Nursing. She decided to return because her marriage had ended and she needed to earn some money. She left the profession twelve years ago, and she lacked confidence and up-to-date knowledge. The course helped her with both these things. She is now a staff nurse working on a children's ward.

Not every nurse's experience is like this one. There is a wide variation in the quality and relevance of the courses themselves. Many authorities are still unable to provide the flexibility of work arrangements required and there is not always a job at the end of the line.

> *Modupe's one disappointment came at the end of her*
> *Back to Nursing course, when she learnt that there*
> *were no part-time posts available to suit the hours she*
> *could work.*

The Open College has recently launched a major new Return to Nursing initiative designed to provide open learning resources for the core curriculum of a Return to Nursing course. For more details contact the Open College. For further details on Return to Nursing courses contact the English National Board for Nursing, Midwifery and Health Visiting, Careers Advisory Centre. There are similar centres in Scotland, Northern Ireland and Wales (see the end of the chapter).

LAW

Law is not an area which is currently facing a skills shortage, but it is one field which is increasingly recognising the importance of retaining highly trained staff. As one lawyer said,

> *If women work hard and get through the exams we*
> *need to make sure that we don't lose them.*

The Association of Women Solicitors runs an annual eight-day Returner course, aimed at women and men who are returning to law after an absence (cost £350). There is also a growing interest from several of the Polytechnics and Universities, and it's likely that more will be available in coming years.

- *Newcastle Polytechnic* runs a Returner course, half a day a week for several weeks.
- *Bristol and Leeds Polytechnics* run a 'Return to Legal Practice' course.
- *Leicester University* runs an eight-week course with a placement with a local firm.

The Law College is looking at how correspondence courses can be adapted for women returners (correspondence courses in Scots Law are not available at present). For details of Returner courses, contact The Law Society and ask for a copy of *The Guide to Continuing Education*, where all returner/refresher training is listed. In Scotland, contact The Law Society of Scotland for details.

For information about support groups, see the end of this chapter.

WHAT WILL IT COST TO STUDY OR TRAIN?

For many women the cost of education and training is high and this, combined with the practical hurdles of childcare and domestic responsibilities, has made it almost impossible for a large number of women to take up educational opportunities.

In some of the other countries in Europe a lot more public money is spent on education and training. It is likely that the UK situation won't be improving either. Some adult education courses may be cut due to the implementation of the Poll Tax, and by creating the TECs, it is clear that the Government wants to pass the responsibility for vocational education and training and its costs to employers and individuals.

However, a certain amount of public funding for education and training does, at present, exist and in addition, because employers are worried about the lack of skilled people available, they too are investing more money in training.

The cost of courses varies a great deal. Some of the courses I have mentioned in this chapter are free but these are exceptions rather than the rule. You will find that whatever you do it will cost something as there are always hidden costs, such as the price of books and travel. It is a good idea to work out all the different things you will need to pay for and find out what financial help you are entitled to before committing yourself to a course.

WHAT WILL YOU NEED MONEY FOR?

COURSE FEES
Fees can vary a great deal from a few pounds to well over a thousand a year for a full-time postgraduate course. Course costs are almost always given in a publicity leaflet or the college prospectus. If not, ring the college to find out.

EXAM FEES
Some courses involve exams and you may have to pay exam fees separately from your course fee. Again, this fee can vary. If you take a full-time course at a University, Polytechnic or Local Authority College, you may be eligible for a grant to cover course and exam fees. You should be able to find out about exams and fees in the college prospectus. If not, ring the college.

BOOKS AND EQUIPMENT
Whatever you do you will need basic supplies, such as paper and pens. It may not be possible to borrow the books you need from the library so you may be asked to buy books. This can be expensive. Find out from your course tutor or trainer about the cost of books and equipment.

TRAVEL COSTS

If you do a course at a college you will have to pay travel costs to get there and back. Some of the courses I have mentioned give help with travel costs but this is very rare. Work these costs out before committing yourself to a course – they can add up to quite a lot of money.

CHILDCARE COSTS

Some courses help with the cost of childcare – but not many. Whatever arrangements you are able to make, be aware of the costs and plan for these.

As well as the cost of your course you will have to cover all the other costs you would normally have, such as housing, food and bills. You will need to think about these when you budget for your course. If you are on unemployment or supplementary benefit, you should find out whether you will be able to do the course and receive your benefit (see 21-hour rule, page 85).

Most Local Education Authorities offer reduced fees to unemployed or single people and other groups – many married women are excluded because they do not count as unemployed because their husband works.

WHAT FINANCIAL HELP IS AVAILABLE?

The amount of financial help available varies and depends on a number of factors, such as the length of the course, whether you have studied before, the number of hours you study each week and your personal circumstances. In the *New Start Pack* produced by Thames Television, the following general points about financial help are given.

> 1   *If you are on benefits, you may get help with course fees. Some courses may be free to you.*

2 On some full-time courses, you may get an award which will pay your fees and help to cover living expenses. From 1990, a new system of student loans is planned. If you intend to embark upon a full-time course of higher education, find out about this.

3 Students on part-time courses do not get help towards living expenses, but may get help for study expenses such as travel and books.

4 In some cases, students may claim an allowance for childcare.

5 Trainees on ET get a small allowance in addition to any benefits they are receiving. Single parents can claim childcare costs.

The best advice is to get help locally; your Educational Guidance or Careers Service should be able to give you information about how much a course costs and whether you are likely to get a grant. The National Union of Students should be able to give information about student loans (see address list).

GRANTS

In England and Wales there are basically two types of grant available for study from your Local Education Authority. These are Mandatory grants and Discretionary grants.

MANDATORY GRANTS

These are awards which the authority has to give to people who are eligible for specific 'designated' courses. They are for students taking full-time courses in higher education (post A-levels) such as:

- Degree course
- Diploma of Higher Education
- BTEC/HND
- An initial teaching qualification

● Other courses which are thought of by the DES to be comparable to first degrees.

You will only be eligible if you have not previously received a grant for full-time higher education. The rules for eligibility are complex and it is not possible to spell them all out in this chapter. You should contact your Local Education Authority for information about grants (the address and telephone number should be in the phone book under your local Council).

DISCRETIONARY GRANTS

These are normally for full-time further education (up to A-level and its equivalent) such as:

● Access courses
● Full time A-level or similar
● BTEC diploma
● Full-time GCSE.

The Local Education Authority does not have to give these awards. It is up to them to decide. Each Local Education Authority has a different policy, so contact them to find out if you will qualify. In Wales, the Welsh Joint Education Committee will provide information (see address list).

In Scotland, there are two bodies from which funding may be obtained for full-time courses – which you apply to depends on the type of course you are taking. The Scottish Education Department, SED, awards grants for higher education courses which require SCE Highers (usually at least three) for entry. These are mandatory awards and are for similar courses to those listed under 'Mandatory grants' for England and Wales.

As in England and Wales the rules are quite complex but the SED produces a free booklet on grants (*Guide to Student Allowances*) and most regions have leaflets outlining their policies on bursaries. Regional Education Departments award bursaries which are discretionary for full-time courses leading to SCEs, SCOTVEC, National and Higher National Certificates and for Access courses. If you are in doubt, contact the appropriate authority to see if you are eligible.

In Northern Ireland, grants are available from the Education and Library Board. The Department of Education for Northern Ireland produces a free booklet called *Grants to Students* – this should give you further help.

MATURE STUDENT GRANTS
(OLDER STUDENTS' ALLOWANCE)

This allowance supplements the main rate of grant given to students. To qualify, you must be at least 26 years old and have earned over £12 000 in the three years prior to the course.

FELLOWSHIPS

There are a very small number of fellowships (study awards) available for women. These are mainly for professional women returners wanting to re-enter areas such as science, engineering and technology. *The Directory of Education and Training* produced by the Women Returners Network lists details of fellowships in great detail.

POSTGRADUATE COURSES

There are limited funds for Postgraduate study available from the Department of Education, your Local Education Authority or appropriate Research Council. Some Post-graduate courses are supported by the The Department of Employment (Training, Enterprise and Education Directorate) (TEED).

21-HOUR RULE

If you receive Income Support or Unemployment Benefit, you will not be able to attend a full-time further education or higher education course and continue to receive your benefit. If you have been on benefit for at least three months you will be able to do a part-time course for up to 21 hours a week, provided you will give up the course if a job is found for you. Lots of colleges are now providing courses which are under 21 hours. However, availability for work testing is now strictly adhered to and unemployed people are required to prove genuine work availability. You must be able to prove that the course enhances your skills and that you are taking serious steps to find work. If you need help and advice, contact your local Educational Guidance or Careers Service.

WHERE TO GET HELP AND ADVICE ABOUT GRANTS

Contact your Local or Regional Education Authority or Education Department (DES, SED, DENI) for information about grants. Or you could try:

- The Educational Grants Advisory Service
- The National Union of Students
- Your local Educational Guidance Service
- Citizens Advice Bureau.

WHAT IF YOU DON'T GET FINANCIAL HELP?

Students do not have a legal right of appeal either against refusal of an award or against the amount offered. Nevertheless, most Local Education Authorities have a procedure for reconsidering decisions. Write to your Local Education Authority or Education Department. You may be able to apply to a hardship or access fund at the institution where you are studying. This is a small amount of money put aside for Further Education, graduate and postgraduate study. Ask at your college to find out more. You may be able to get a bank loan or a scholarship from an educational trust or charity – ask at your Educational Guidance Service. In Scotland, the SED holds a database of Educational Endowments which can sometimes help students not eligible for mandatory awards. Here's how one woman was helped by her Educational Guidance Service.

Ayo has been living in this country for a number of years, and has two children. She originally went along to her Educational Guidance Service to enquire about training to be a nurse, but after talking to an adviser she decided to do an Access course which would lead her to a Degree in Social Sciences. The adviser was able to give her help with her applications for degree courses, and to trusts and companies for financial help to buy books for her studies and for travel to college.

CONCLUSION

Education and training can offer many things – the chance to stretch yourself, broaden your horizons, change direction and re-train. It can offer you the opportunity to make new friends, share things with people who have just the same worries and fears, develop new confidence and eventually go into something better than you ever dared hope for. For lots of women it has been many of these things. We hope that it will be for you too.

FURTHER INFORMATION

USEFUL ADDRESSES

ADVICE AND INFORMATION
CAREERS FOR WOMEN
2 Valentine Place, London SE1 8QH
Tel: (071) 401 2280

TRAINING ACCESS POINTS (TAPs)
TAP Unit, St Mary's House, c/o Moorfoot,
Sheffield S1 4PQ
Tel: (0742) 597344
WOMEN RETURNERS' PROJECT
System Applied Technology Ltd, Sheffield Science Park,
Howard Street, Sheffield S1 2LX
Tel: (0742) 768682

MAKING A NEW START
HILLCROFT COLLEGE
South Bank, Surbiton, Surrey KT6 6DF
Tel: (081) 399 2688
LUCY CAVENDISH COLLÈGE
Lady Margaret Road, Cambridge CB3 0BU
Tel: (0023) 332190
THE OPEN COLLEGE
101 Wigmore Street, London W1H 9AE
Tel: (071) 935 8088
THE OPEN COLLEGE (SCOTLAND)
Atlantic Chambers, 45 Hope Street, Glasgow G2 6AE
Tel: (041) 248 3492
THE OPEN UNIVERSITY
The Central Enquiry Service, PO Box 71, Milton Keynes
MK7 6AG
Tel: (0908) 653231

UPDATING YOUR SKILLS
Banking

WOMEN IN BANKING
55 Bourne Vale, Hayes, Bromley, Kent
BR2 7NU
Contact group for women already in Banking. Please
write, marking correspondence 'Women in
Banking'.   Contact: Ann Leverett.

Computing

BROOK STREET BUREAU
Tel: (0727) 48292   Contact: Mrs Williams
NATIONAL COMPUTING CENTRE UK
Oxford House, Oxford Road, Manchester M1 7ED
Tel: (061) 228 6333
THE WOMEN'S TRAINING NETWORK
161 Harehills Lane, Leeds LS8 3QE
Tel: (0532) 499031

Computing Support Groups

THE ASSOCIATION OF PERSONAL ASSISTANTS AND SECRETARIES
14 Victoria Terrace, Royal Leamington Spa, Warwickshire
CV31 3AB
Tel: (0926) 424844/424794
WOMEN INTO COMPUTING GROUP
Staff Development Officer, Staff Development Service,
University of Glasgow, Glasgow G12 8QQ   Contact:
Helen Watt
Tel: (041) 339 8855 x4270
WOMEN INTO INFORMATION TECHNOLOGY FOUNDATION
Concept 2000, 250 Farnborough Road, Farnborough, Hants
GU14 7LU
Tel: (0252) 528329
WOMEN'S COMPUTER CENTRE
Wesley House, 4 Wild Court, Off Kingsway, London
WC2B 5AU
Tel: (071) 430 0112

Engineering

THE UNIVERSITY OF LIVERPOOL
Research Unit, Engineering Professors' Conference,
PO Box 147, Liverpool L69 3BX

Engineering Support Groups

THE ENGINEERING COUNCIL
10 Maltravers Street, London WC2R 3ER
Tel: (071) 240 7891
WOMEN IN ENGINEERING CENTRE
c/o Dept of Electrical Engineering, South Bank
Polytechnic, London SE1 0AA
Tel: (071) 928 8989 x2042
THE WOMEN'S ENGINEERING SOCIETY
c/o Dept of Civil Engineering, Imperial College of Science
& Technology, Imperial College Road, London SW7 2BU
Tel: (071) 589 5111 x4731

Industrial Management

CRANFIELD INSTITUTE OF TECHNOLOGY
College of Manufacturing, Cranfield, Bedford MK43 0AL
Tel: (0234) 750111 x2640/2650
Manufacturing Management Course aimed at women
returners.
UNIVERSITY OF BRADFORD
Department of Industrial Technology, Bradford, West
Yorkshire BD7 1DP
Tel: (0274) 733466 x8424
Manufacturing Management Course for women returners.

Industrial Management Support Group

WOMEN INTO INDUSTRY
130 Brighton Road, Hooley, Coulsdon, Surrey CR2 3EF
Please write marking your correspondence 'Women into
Industry'.

Law

THE LAW SOCIETY
113 Chancery Lane, London WC2A 1PL
Tel: (071) 242 1222
THE LAW SOCIETY (SCOTLAND)
Law Society's Hall, PO Box 1, Drumsleugh Gardens,
Edinburgh EH3 7YR
Tel: (031) 226 7411

Manual Trades

WOMEN IN CONSTRUCTION ADVISORY GROUP
Room 182, South Bank House, Black Prince Road, London
SE1 7SJ
Tel: (071) 587 1802
WOMEN AND MANUAL TRADES
52/54 Featherstone Street, London EC1Y 8RT
Tel: (071) 251 9192

Nursing

ENGLISH NATIONAL BOARD FOR NURSING, MIDWIFERY & HEALTH
VISITING
Victory House, 170 Tottenham Court Road, London
W1P 0HA
Tel: (071) 388 3131

NURSING IN NORTHERN IRELAND
RAC House, 79 Chichester Street, Belfast BT1 4JE
Tel: (0232) 238152
NURSING IN SCOTLAND
22 Queen Street, Edinburgh EH2 1JX
Tel: (031) 226 7371
NURSING IN WALES
13th Floor, Pearl Assurance House, Greyfriars Road,
Cardiff CF1 3AG
Tel: (0222) 395535

Teaching

TASC – TEACHING AS A CAREER UNIT
Elizabeth House, York Road, London SE1 7PH

OTHER SUPPORT GROUPS
THE ASSOCIATION OF SOLICITORS
See Law Society Address
ASSOCIATION OF WOMEN IN PUBLIC RELATIONS
c/o Granard Rowland Communications, 4–12 Lower
Regent Street, London SW1Y 4PE   Contact: Jane Atkinson
MEDICAL WOMEN'S FEDERATION
Tavistock House North, Tavistock Square, London
WC1H 9HX
Tel: (071) 387 7765
NATIONAL ASSOCIATION OF WOMEN PHARMACISTS
1 Lambeth High Street, London SE1 7JN
Please write, marking your correspondence 'National
Association of Women Pharmacists'.
WOMEN ARCHITECTS' GROUP
66 Portland Place, London W1N 4AD
WOMEN IN DENTISTRY
The Surgery, Orchard Lane, Crewkerne, Somerset
TA18 7AT
Please write, marking your correspondence 'Women in
Dentistry'.
WOMEN IN ENTERTAINMENT
11 Acklan Road, London W10
Please write, marking your correspondence 'Women in
Entertainment'.
WOMEN IN LIBRARIES
Wesley House, Wild Court, London WC2B 5AU
Please write, marking your correspondence 'Women in
Libraries'.

WOMEN IN MANAGEMENT
64 Marryat Road, Wimbledon, London SW19 5BN
Tel: (081) 944 6332
WOMEN IN MEDICINE
15 Lyons Fold, Sale, Cheshire M33 1LF
Please write, marking your correspondence 'Women in Medicine'.
WOMEN IN PHYSICS
47 Belgrave Square, London SW1X 8QX
Tel: (071) 235 6111
WOMEN IN PUBLISHING
Information Officer, c/o *The Bookseller*, 12 Dyott Street, London WC1A 1DF
WOMEN IN THE CIVIL SERVICE
DTI, Personnel Management Division, Allington Towers, 19 Allington Street, London SW1E 5EB
Tel: (071) 215 5000

THE COSTS OF EDUCATION AND TRAINING
THE DEPARTMENT OF EDUCATION AND SCIENCE (DES)
Elizabeth House, York Road, London SE1 7PH
Tel: (071) 934 9000
THE DEPARTMENT OF EDUCATION FOR NORTHERN IRELAND (DENI)
Rathgael House, Balloo Road, Bangor, County Down BT19 2PR
Tel: (0247) 270077
THE SCOTTISH EDUCATION DEPARTMENT (SED)
Haymarket House, Clifton Terrace, Edinburgh EH12 5DT
Tel: (031) 556 8400
THE DES IN WALES
Welsh Joint Education Committee, 245 Western Avenue, Cardiff CF5 2YY
Tel: (0222) 561231

EDUCATIONAL GRANTS ADVISORY SERVICE
Students Advisor, Family Welfare Association,
501/505 Kingsland Road, Dalston, London E8 4AU
Tel: (071)254 6251
NATIONAL UNION OF STUDENTS
Grants Department, 461 Holloway Road, London N7 6LJ
Tel: (071) 272 8900

USEFUL BOOKS

- *Directory of Education and Training Opportunities for Women in Wales*
  Contact: REPLAN, Cardiff (0222) 561231, free of charge
- *New Start*, Thames Television plc in association with the National Educational Guidance Initiative, UDACE
- *Returning to Work*, Kogan Page
  A directory of education and training for women by the Women Returners Network
- *Second Chances*, Andrew Pates and Martin Good, COIC
  A national guide to adult education and training
- *Second Chance in Scotland,* SIACE
  A woman's guide to education and training
  Contact: SIACE (031) 229 0331
- *Start Again*, Equal Opportunities Commission for Northern Ireland
  Contact: Equal Opportunities Commission for N. Ireland (0232) 242752, free of charge
- *Fresh Start*, Thames Television plc in association with the Open College

THREE

GETTING A

JOB

ANN SEDLEY

Ann Sedley is a specialist in equal opportunity practice and has been engaged in equal opportunities work in the voluntary, public and private sectors for 11 years.

In addition, she has published material on part-time workers, sex discrimination law, sexual harassment, and recruitment and retention issues.

Ann is a USA German Marshall Fund Equal Opportunity Fellow and currently works in London as a personnel officer responsible for recruitment and retention.

INTRODUCTION

There have been some significant changes in employment practice over the last few years. These have led to a more systematic approach to recruitment and selection and are the result of a greater awareness of the importance of equal treatment for women in the workplace. They should benefit women who are thinking of returning to paid work after a break because they require the employer to look at an individual's skills and abilities to do a job rather than the stereotypical image they might have because they are mothers or single parents. There is also a growing awareness of the important contribution that women make when they return to paid work after taking a break. More employers are realising that they need their skills and talents and are making a greater effort to attract them.

But despite advances being made in employment practice and changing attitudes, getting a job is often not easy. You may be lucky enough to be offered the first job you apply for, but you may find that you have to apply for a number of jobs before being offered one. Job hunting can be a difficult and painful process, one which may involve you feeling rejected and frustrated, and at times like giving up completely. But it is important to keep going – even if your search proves very difficult. You will find that you become more adept at reading job adverts, skimming the newspapers and filling in application forms. You may even find that the whole process of job hunting helps you to clarify what it is you really want to do. Going to interviews can provide a real insight into working life, and one which can help you define more clearly what you want to do and where you want to work.

This chapter is about how you can go about getting a job. It starts by giving guidance about how to reassess your situation and how to find out about vacancies. Then it goes on to give information about how to apply for jobs and advice on how to prepare yourself for an interview, so that you give the interviewers all the information they need about you. It also looks at some of the ways that employment procedures have changed in the last few years, including equal opportunity practices, which should help to ensure that women get a fairer chance.

A TIME TO REASSESS

Now you are beginning to think about getting a job, it is a very good time to review your interests and think about what sort of work you would like to do. You might decide to go back to the work you were doing before you took a break. But on the other hand it might be a good time to think about doing something completely different. Chapter 2 looked at organisations which can help with these decisions.

You will also need to assess your own requirements from a job. Hours of work, holiday entitlement, salary, prospects and location will be of great practical importance. These are big decisions and it may take some careful thought to come up with answers.

This is where you can start involving your family and

friends in your decision to return to work. Talk to them about the sort of job you might look for. If you feel like a change, but you are not sure what to change to, think about the things you like doing now, either at home, as a hobby or in a voluntary capacity, as well as the skills you have learned and enjoyed while you have not been employed. Make a list of all these things and see if it gives you any ideas when you look through job advertisements. If you are not sure what kind of employment they might lead to then get some advice (see chapter 2).

RECOGNISING YOUR SKILLS

It is very important to recognise and believe in your own skills and abilities. This is not an easy thing to do and many women do not value the things they can do and have done. It is really worth spending quite a lot of time on this when you are preparing to apply for a job. Work with a friend or friends, think through all the jobs you have done, both paid and unpaid, and the skills that you have developed in doing them. Here are some examples of the skills you may have developed through doing different kinds of unpaid work.

VOLUNTARY AND COMMUNITY WORK

This could include being involved in your tenants association, or school fund-raising, or visiting an older person. All of these indicate skills and abilities such as:

- team working
- budgeting
- organisational and caring skills

Consider how these skills might be transferable and useful in the paid work environment or to a particular job.

BEING A MOTHER

Think about the skills you have learned as a result of being at home with children – many of them will be transferable to the workplace. For example:

CARING SKILLS
You will have developed these through:

– looking after children
– first aid
– cooking
– counselling

COMMUNICATION SKILLS
– communicating with children, playgroup leaders, teachers, other parents

WORKING TO DEADLINES
– getting children to school on time

ORGANISATIONAL/MANAGEMENT AND PLANNING SKILLS
– running a home
– doing the shopping before the baby needs feeding
– planning meals
– arranging children's social life

BUDGETING SKILLS
– shopping
– bills
– family budget

ABILITY TO PRIORITISE AND BE FLEXIBLE
- coping with several things at once
- deciding what to do first
- adapting to a variety of demands

It's been worked out that if women were paid for being at home looking after their family, they would earn about £20,000 a year. So don't undervalue yourself.

You must be able to convince yourself of your own worth so that you can convince others. Remember that prospective employers do not know you, you have to tell them about yourself in a positive and honest way. This is not boasting, it is giving information.

ATTITUDES

Not only will you have to convince a prospective employer that you are the right person for the job, but you may well have to overcome hostile attitudes at home and convince your family that it is a good idea for you to return to paid work.

The people close to you have probably got used to having you around all the time and ensuring that their lives run smoothly. Now it's your turn to go out into the big wide world, they will need to give you some support. And they may have to take on some of the domestic chores which you have always done.

Lots of people find change difficult to contemplate, whether at home, school, or work. And your decision to look for a job is no different. It involves change – both for you and for your family. There are a number of ways to make this sort of change easier for everyone and therefore to try to ensure that you don't experience negative attitudes from your family. It is important to involve your family in the decision right from the start. Once you have decided, for whatever reason, that you are interested in looking for a job, talk to your family about it. Explain why you want to do it. Discuss the changes it might mean for everyone. A lot of the changes will be positive.

Your reasons will no doubt include earning money which will probably ease things financially and improve life for everyone. They may include the fact that you are feeling bored at home and you will feel less bored and be more interesting with contacts and activities outside the home. Your reasons may include wanting to use the training and skills which you developed before having a family. You will therefore be benefiting the community as a whole by putting them to use again. You will find that whatever your reason for wanting to return to paid work, there will be a positive spinoff for the people close to you. Share that with them.

During this period of discussion, listen to their fears about your return to work. Take them seriously, then deal with them. Discuss their fears and if there are practical difficulties work out together how they can be managed.

But during this time of involving others in your decision try not to forget you are a person in your own right and you are entitled to make decisions for yourself about what you want to do with your life. This is not always easy, especially as so many women have been conditioned to care for others and put themselves second. But sometimes it is important to fight this conditioning and stand up for yourself.

The Midland Bank has published a Charter to help women think through the demands of home and work. You might find it useful as you plan to return.

1   I am not on call to all of the people all of the time.
2   I have needs of my own which may not be the same as my family's, my colleagues' or my friends'.
3   I do not have to say 'yes' to every request made of me.

4   I do not have to carry on doing something just because I've always done it.
5   Time spent relaxing is time well spent.
6   There is no such thing as the 'perfect mother', 'perfect wife' or 'perfect child'.
7   Time spent feeling guilty could be time spent doing more enjoyable things.
8   I shouldn't always do it for them if they are capable of doing it for themselves.
9   I should give myself the same time, care and consideration that I give to others.
10 I should remember at all times, especially in the face of criticism, difficulties and anxiety . . . I am doing the best I can.

WHERE DO YOU FIND JOB VACANCIES?

Now you have decided to look for a job, and thought about what sort of job you want, you must find out where the vacancies are. This might sound obvious, but it's not always straightforward. Lots of jobs are advertised but there are also lots of jobs that are not. If they are not advertised you will have to go out and find them.

JOBS THAT ARE ADVERTISED

Job advertisements should give the job title, location, salary and some information about the employing organisation as well as job details. But not all advertisements provide all this information. If they don't, you could ring up to ask for the details you need.

Jobs are advertised in many different places. Where they are advertised may depend on their geographical location, whether the organisation will be recruiting locally, or nationally, what sort of job it is, unskilled, skilled, professional and so on.

If you are looking for a local job, you might try:

- **Your local Job Centre** – Call in regularly as new jobs come in frequently.
- **Your local newspaper** – Check the Situations Vacant pages on the day it comes out.
- **Free magazines** – These often carry job advertisements and are sometimes published by your local council on a regular day of the week. Check them every week.
- **Newsagent's window** – This is often a useful source of adverts for jobs such as gardening and cleaning.
- **Your local library** – There is often a notice-board advertising jobs; you might also advertise your skills as well. Some job-hunters try to make their availability known by placing advertisements about themselves in newspapers or journals.
- **Private employment agencies** – You will find these in most high streets, or look them up in the telephone directory or Yellow Pages.

Remember, if you do not find what you want the first time you look, don't give up. Sometimes looking at job advertisements for a while can help you decide what you want to do, as one woman found out.

> *I found it very useful to look at job adverts regularly for a few weeks to see what sort of jobs were coming up and to help me decide what I could do. It helped me decide that I wanted to work in the public sector and that I was capable of applying for jobs in a particular salary range.*

If you are looking for jobs in more specialised areas or professions you might try:

THE NATIONAL PRESS

The *Guardian* advertises different categories of jobs on different days. For instance it advertises media related jobs on Monday, education jobs on Tuesday, public appointments including local authority jobs on Wednesday, computer and new technology jobs on Thursday and repeats many of them at the weekend in a special supplement. The *Independent* and the *Daily Telegraph* also carry appointments columns as do the Sunday papers. *The Times* has a 'Crème de la Crème' section on Wednesday which advertises secretarial jobs.

THE ETHNIC COMMUNITY PRESS

More employers, particularly those with an equal opportunity policy, are advertising posts in what is known as the Ethnic Community Press. You might be interested in looking in the *Caribbean Times*, the *Voice* or the *Asian Times* or one of the other more local papers. For more details contact your local community relations council or the Commission for Racial Equality (see the address list at the end of this chapter).

SPECIALISED AND PROFESSIONAL PRESS

Jobs in particular specialised areas or professions will often be advertised in the specialist press and trade journals. For example, if you are interested in working in local governments, look in the *Local Government Chronicle*. If you are interested in working in the National Health Service, try the *Health Service Journal* or *Nursing Times*. *Personnel Management* and *Personnel Today* include advertisements for jobs in personnel and human resource management. There are other specialist journals covering many crafts, trades and professions. You will find these magazines in big newsagents (you may have to order them specially) and sometimes in your local library or through subscribing to the relevant professional or trade association.

JOBS THAT ARE NOT ADVERTISED

For those jobs which are not advertised, it is a matter of doing some detective work and promoting yourself in a different way. Once you have decided what sort of job you want, talk to people you know who do that type of work, or to careers advisers to find out what sort of organisation you should contact. You can ask people you know if they know of vacancies. You can also telephone or write to organisations 'on spec' i.e. without knowing if vacancies exist. Ask to speak to the personnel officer or the person who deals with recruitment. Otherwise you could write, enclosing your CV, asking whether they have any vacancies, whether they are likely to have any, and to put your name on a list or send you details. Here's how one woman researched an area which interested her and got interviews:

> When I decided that I wanted to work in a
> photographic studio, I looked up 'photographic studios'
> in the Yellow Pages and found there were about 150. I
> chose the ones in the areas where I wanted to work,
> wrote a letter and photocopied it. Then I got my family
> to help me address the envelopes. I also enclosed a
> copy of my CV. I got lots of replies, most saying they
> had no vacancies, but a few asked me to come for
> interview.

EMPLOYMENT AGENCIES

Employment agencies are often found in High Streets of larger towns. Many employment agencies specialise, for instance in accountancy, secretarial work, nursing, catering or legal work. But many offer temporary or permanent work in a range of occupations. Some give free training in new technology. They provide a free service to job applicants.

APPLYING FOR A JOB

DOING THE PREPARATION

If you are interested in applying for an advertised job, you should write or phone for further information and an application form. Employers vary a great deal in how much information they send out to prospective employees. Some employers will send information about conditions of service (salary, or wages, holidays, pensions and so on) and details of the job (job description). You may also be sent a person specification.

The job description and person specification help you to decide if you really want to apply for the job, and whether you have the right qualifications, experience, skills and abilities for it. They will also help you to complete the application form.

WHAT IS A JOB DESCRIPTION?

A job description should state the purpose of the post and give some background to it. It should list all the tasks involved. Sometimes it will say which are the most important tasks in the job. It should also explain who the job holder's manager will be, whether the job holder will be managing anyone and how the job fits into the department or organisation.

WHAT IS A
PERSON SPECIFICATION?

A person specification is a description of the characteristics that a person needs to do the job. The characteristics are usually divided under different headings such as qualifications, or education and training, knowledge, experience, skills and abilities, other requirements and sometimes personal qualities. Each heading should be broken down into different criteria which match the tasks in the job description. Each criterion should be clearly defined so that applicants and selectors know what is meant. Sometimes there will be a further sub-division into 'essential' and 'desirable' criteria. Essential criteria are those that are definitely required if the job is to be done effectively. Desirable criteria are extra, but might be looked at if there are a large number of applicants who meet the essential criteria.

The person specification can be very helpful to you because you can match your skills, abilities, experience and qualifications etc to those described in the person specification.

WHAT SHOULD I DO IF THERE IS NO PERSON SPECIFICATION?

Unfortunately, many employers do not use person specifications. You might find it useful to try and draw one up yourself to give you an idea of what requirements might be relevant. This would be a rough guide to help you complete the application form, and remember that it will only be a rough guess. You will not have all the necessary inside information to do a thorough job and it will not be a document that the employer will be using in the selection process.

If you want to try putting your own person specification together, look at the job description and highlight the tasks described in it. Then, on a large sheet of paper put five headings:

1 Education/Training/Qualifications
2 Skills/Abilities
3 Knowledge
4 Experience
5 Other

Under each heading note down what you think might be required for the job. Ask a friend to help you – two brains are often better than one. You might not put anything under one or two headings. For instance, if it's a first-level clerical job, you might not require any qualifications. If it's a gardening job you might need horticultural qualifications or you might just need the experience and knowledge you have gained from looking after your own garden. If it's an accountancy or engineering job, you will need to have the appropriate qualifications.

APPLICATION FORMS

PREPARING TO FILL IN THE APPLICATION FORM

It is worthwhile spending some time preparing to fill in the application form. You can always use the information for other job applications. It is not time wasted! As one woman said:

> When I went for this job with the council, I hadn't filled in an application form for years. Someone suggested that I write down everything I had done and the skills and knowledge I had learned from them – jobs and voluntary work and the things I have done with the kids. It took me a long time, but when I had done it I was very impressed and thought 'Is this really me?' Anyway, it was time well spent, because when I looked at what the job involved, it was much easier to explain on the application form why I had the necessary skills and experience to do the job, including a lot of things I had forgotten about.

Here is a checklist of steps to take when preparing to fill in an application form:

1 Make a rough draft listing your education and qualifications, all the jobs you have had in the past and the voluntary work you have done as well as domestic, social and other activities.

2 Check it through with someone who knows you well to make sure you have not forgotten anything.

3 Write down, in rough, the experience that you gained from each job or activity, the skills and abilities you learned and knowledge you have gained. You will be surprised to find how skilled you are! For example:
   – *Travel*: organisational skills, communication skills, planning, finance and so on;
   – *Childcare*: organisational and planning skills, communication, motivation, managerial skills, time-management, budgeting etc;
   – *Shopworker*: numeracy, communication skills, speed, accuracy and so on.

4 Match your skills, abilities and knowledge etc to those in the person specification, your own made-up person specification, the job description or job advertisement, if you can. A lot of the skills you have gained will be transferable to different situations.

5 Give examples of things you have done or knowledge you have gained to back up the information you are giving. Write in a positive way, 'I was responsible for . . .', 'I planned . . .', 'I have an interest in . . .'. Specify the things you have done rather than things the unit, office or department has done.

FILLING IN THE APPLICATION FORM

You will be asked to give information about your education and employment history on the application form.

HOBBIES AND INTERESTS

Some forms include a space for information about your hobbies and interests. Highlight those that you have already identified as giving you skills and experience that will help you to do the job you are applying for. For example:

- Minutes secretary of community association.
- Parent Teacher Association – treasurer and jumble sale organiser.

WHY YOU ARE THE BEST PERSON FOR THE JOB

The most important part of the application form is the part where you explain why you want the job and give details of your experience, skills and other relevant information. This is where you use your rough draft and give information about your past employment and other experience, matching each point to the requirements in the person specification or advertisement or the different parts of the job description. This is where you can describe the experience and skills you have developed at home. For example if it's an office job requiring team work and organisational and planning skills, you can give, as an example of your ability to work in a team, the fact that you have run a family for so many years and you could describe some of the issues like this:

TEAM WORKING SKILLS

- *support* (i.e. caring for and listening to your children)
- making *collective agreements*, like what you will all do at the weekend
- *negotiating procedures* (such as children's bedtimes).

These also indicate organisational and planning skills as do so many other domestic tasks.

Give examples and don't forget that the selectors don't know anything about you, you must give them the information.

They cannot guess and you should not leave them to make assumptions.

You might find that there is not enough room in the space provided to say all you want to say. Don't worry, just use a blank piece of paper to complete your answer and attach it to the form.

REFERENCES

Most employers ask applicants to give the name of one or two referees, people who can verify your work record or who know you personally and can confirm that you are who you say you are. The employer will then contact them at some point in the selection procedure.

Some employers use references to help them make a decision about who to appoint, others treat them more as a formality. However, you do not know what value will be placed on the reference, so make sure you think carefully about who you should name. Consider the following points:

- If an employer's reference is required, make sure you name a manager or supervisor who can give the necessary information about your work.
- If a personal reference is needed, give the name of someone who knows you well.
- If you have not been employed for some time and cannot give an employer reference, give the name of someone who can testify to your abilities and if necessary explain why you have not given an employer's name.
- Don't forget to ask the permission of the referees to use their names before you put them on the form.
- If you would prefer, for any reason, that references are not taken up unless you are about to be offered the job, say so on the form.

COVERING LETTERS TO ACCOMPANY APPLICATION FORMS

Once you have completed the application form, make sure you send it with a covering letter to the organisation within the time limit given. It is likely that your application form will have asked for all the information that the employer needs to know, so your covering letter could be quite brief, and just state the post you are applying for and where you saw it advertised. You may feel that you want to draw the employer's attention to something in particular; perhaps you have recently completed a course which is relevant to the job – there is no harm in doing this if you want to. There is an example of the sort of letter you might send with an application form opposite.

Points to remember, when you are completing your form:
- Use a typewriter if you have got one.
- Use black ink, if you don't have a typewriter, and write clearly – application forms are often photocopied.
- Check your spelling and punctuation.

3 September 1990

8 The Grove
Darton
Lincolnshire LN5 6YT

THE PERSONNEL MANAGER
HOADLEY & CO.
60–61 PEMBERTON ROAD
DARTON
LINCOLNSHIRE LN5 7AP

Dear Sir or Madam

I enclose my application form for the post of Office Manager as advertised in last week's *Lincs Chronicle*.

I hope that my skills and experience will make me suitable for consideration.

I look forward to hearing from you.

Your faithfully

Sarah Castleton

- Make a copy of the application form for yourself so that you can remind yourself what you have written if you are called for an interview.
- Allow at least four days for delivery in the mail or deliver it by hand. Remember, late applications are often not considered.

PREPARING A CURRICULUM VITAE (CV)°

A CV or Curriculum Vitae is the document which sets out all the information about you which an employer will need to know in order to consider you for a job. It includes all the information that you would put on a job application form, but is more general and wide ranging because it is not geared to one particular job. It will give your name and address, work experience, list your key skills and abilities, your education, and any qualifications you have. You might also include hobbies and out of work interests if they are relevant to the sort of employment you are interested in.

If you are writing to an employer 'on spec' for information about vacancies, you will need to send a CV to them. Employers often ask for a CV rather than sending an application form for you to complete.

There are companies which will write a CV for you. They advertise in the local and national press. However, if you want to prepare one for yourself, here are some suggestions.

- Make sure it is not too long. Aim for one or two sides of A4 paper. Head the first sheet with your name, address and telephone number.
- Give some information about your education and training, your interests and voluntary work. Then give a brief outline of your previous work experience and the main skills and abilities you bring from each job.
- Either type it out yourself or get a good typist (a friend or a professional) to type it for you. It is important that it is well presented and easy to read. It gives an important impression to an employer about the trouble you are taking with your job hunt.

There are different ways of writing CVs and every book you

look in will suggest a slightly different structure or layout. The most important thing is that you make the most of what you have to offer. There is an example of how you might set out your CV on pp 116–117.

PERSONAL INFORMATION

Strictly speaking there is no need to include personal information in your CV or in your application form. However, in practice, many employers do ask about marital status, number of children and nationality, and not for monitoring purposes. Research and experience have shown that this information can be used to discriminate against women and people from ethnic minorities. For example, some employers think that having young children makes women unreliable employees and will not consider them for jobs. If they do not have that information they are more likely to look at your application on the basis of your skills and abilities. After all, there are lots of things that can make people unreliable, and they do not ask about those! You might decide not to include this information on your CV – as we have done, on the basis that it might be used against you and is not necessary for the selection procedure. If an employer needs to know about personal matters for pension arrangements and so on, he or she can ask that after you have been offered the job.

CURRICULUM VITAE

NAME: Jane Morton
ADDRESS: 45 Angel Street, Northtown,
                   Berkshire BE5 7TY
DATE OF BIRTH: 17–2–1960

EDUCATION & QUALIFICATIONS

1971–1976 St Anne's School for Girls O-level English
                                      CSE maths, typing,
                                      history, biology

Further Education:

1976–1978
Two-year secretarial/business studies at London
Polytechnic.
Subjects included: Typing, word-processing, shorthand,
communications, law, French and accountancy.

WORK EXPERIENCE:

1989–1990

Registered Childminder

Duties: Looking after several small children.
Skills developed: – caring skills
                      – organising and planning skills

1985–1989

Full-time mother

While taking a career break to bring up two childen, I
have developed the following skills:
– caring skills
– organisational and planning skills
– time-management skills
– financial and budgeting skills

1979–1985

Roxborough Borough Council, Legal Department

Position held   **Clerical Officer**

Main duties
- filing, typing, computer input
- team administration, telephone work, memos, taking team meeting minutes

Skills developed
- office management
- communication skills

1978–1979

Wimbourne & Stuart, Solicitors

Position held   **Secretary**

Main duties
- office skills; typing, filing
- office administration
- telephone enquiries

Interests and Voluntary work

I help at the local playgroup and I am secretary of the parents' committee for which I organise the meetings and take minutes. I also organise fund-raising events for the play group. I go to a keep-fit class once a week and enjoy keeping up my window boxes and growing house plants.

REFEREES

Mr John Simpkins	Ms Freda Stuart
Administrator	Partner
Legal Department	Wimbourne & Stuart Solicitors
Roxborough Borough Council	68–72 High Street
Lower Street	Wood Green
Roxborough RX5 2LT	London N22 4UB
Tel: (0652) 83467	Tel: (081) 245 8977

7 December 1990

45 Angel Street
Northtown
Berkshire BE5 7TY

MRS A TILLEY
PERSONNEL MANAGER
NORTHTOWN BOROUGH COUNCIL
CIVIC STREET
NORTHTOWN
BERKSHIRE BE4 8LS

Dear Mrs Tilley

With reference to your advertisement in the 'Evening Herald' on 29th November, I would like to apply for the post of Administrator in the Social Services Department at Northtown Borough Council.

As you can see from my CV I am an experienced organiser and recognise the importance of team work for the smooth running of an office.

I am an efficient worker with good keyboard and computer skills. I am aware of the importance of well organised office systems and careful budgeting. My past experience as Clerical Officer for Roxborough Council has also helped me to develop good communication and management skills.

I would be available to work full-time, but would also like to know if you offer part-time work or job shares.

I hope you will view my application favourably and I look forward to hearing your reply. I shall be available for interview at your convenience.

Yours sincerely

Jane Morton

COVERING LETTERS TO ACCOMPANY A CV

Advice about what to put in this kind of covering letter varies. But as your CV is not likely to be geared specifically to the job you are applying for, you will need to draw out the skills and experience which you want the employer to notice in the letter, especially those which are particularly relevant to the job. Opposite is an example covering letter to accompany a CV.

INTERVIEWS

If you have been asked to go for an interview, it means you have been shortlisted, the employer is interested in you and wants to know more. Interviews can often be quite nerve-racking, but try to view them as an opportunity to give more information about yourself and an opportunity for you to find out more about the organisation you have applied to work for. After all, you might decide you don't like them after you've been for the interview. It is a good idea to approach the interview as though it is a meeting. A good employer will approach it in this way too. However, not all employers will be so enlightened and some will be more heavy handed.

BEFORE THE INTERVIEW

Always prepare for an interview. Think about taking the following steps:

1 Find out about the organisation, what it makes or sells or what the department does, if the job is in a local

authority. You might telephone and ask for this information or maybe ask someone you know who works there,
or in a similar job for a different organisation.

2   Check out how this job fits into the workplace as a whole,
or plan to ask about this at the interview if you have not
been told or cannot find out.

3   Look at the job description and the person specification,
if you have been given one, or your imaginary one if you
have not.

4   Think about the information you want to give about
yourself and the way you would approach the job in question. It doesn't matter if you repeat information at the
interview which you have put in the application form.

5   Think about why you are interested in the job and why
you want to work for that employer.

PREPARING FOR QUESTIONS

Interviewers often ask why you are interested in the job as
an opening question. Write down the main points you would
like to make. Another common opening question is 'Tell me
about yourself'. Again, outline some of your strong points,
particularly those relevant to this job, and try not to ramble
on!

Most questions will concentrate on different aspects of
the job so think about the main points you will make on each
aspect and write them down to help you remember. Always
follow up with an example from your own experience. For
example if you are asked about the importance of teamwork,
you might list some important aspects such as co-operation,
flexibility, cover, in-service training and then follow up with
an example from your own experience of how you found
working in a team important for you. (Your family is a good
example of a team, if you have not had any workplace experience to draw on).

Some interviewers ask hypothetical questions such as if you were faced with a particular issue or problem how do you think you would deal with it? Hypothetical questions are often difficult to answer. If you find it difficult, think back to a similar situation that you have dealt with and use that as a basis for your answer.

Some interviewers ask what are called closed questions, i.e. questions that only call for a 'yes' or 'no' answer. If this happens, you might decide to follow it up with an explanation or an example.

If you are asked a multi-faceted question, i.e. one that requires several answers, don't be afraid to say, 'I'll answer the first part and then maybe you could repeat the second part of the question.'

If you do not understand a question, say so. This is more likely a reflection on the questioner putting a poorly worded or badly thought out question than on your ability to understand it! Ask them to repeat it in a different way.

Always have some questions ready to ask the interview panel. It shows that you are interested in the organisation and the job. You probably want to know more anyway. If you are worried that you will forget the questions you have planned, write them down and take them into the interview with you. You might ask the panel about career development and training opportunities; about the goods that the company manufactures; about how the work of the department fits into the whole organisation; or about terms and conditions that have not been explained to you.

Plan how you are going to get to the interview and how much time you will need. It is better to be early than late. Think about what you are going to wear before the day of the interview so that you have no last-minute panics.

DURING THE INTERVIEW

When you are answering questions try to speak slowly and clearly. If you need a moment to think of the answer, take it. A short silence is all right. If there is more than one person interviewing you, look at the person who asked the question when you answer. Remember that most people feel nervous when they go for interviews. Employers should be aware of this and try to put you at your ease.

AFTER THE INTERVIEW

Most people do not get the first job they apply for. Many people apply for jobs over and over again. So do not give up if you are unsuccessful the first time, but learn from the experience. It can be a good idea to write or phone the organisation to get some feedback on your application and/ or interview. If the organisation has an equal opportunity policy it should have recorded the reasons for selecting and rejecting applicants and be able to help you review your strengths and weaknesses.

If the organisation is not very helpful, think about the aspects of the interview that you felt all right about and those that you did not handle so well. Use the experience to plan how you can improve on these aspects. But whatever you do, do not give up – there is bound to be a job out there which is right for you.

EMPLOYMENT RIGHTS

You might have to bear in mind school hours and holidays when considering what sort of job to apply for. Far more employers are offering different types of flexible working because they want to encourage women to work for them.

Some offer term-time working, shorter hours, or job sharing. If you are thinking of working fewer than full-time hours, whatever the arrangement, it is important to know about your employment rights.

The Employment Protection Consolidation Act (EPCA) gives you protection from unfair dismissal, a right to redundancy payments and the right to maternity leave and pay, if you have worked for the same employer for 2 years for 16 or more hours a week. If you work for between 8 and 16 hours a week, you will have to have worked for 5 years for the same employer before you have these employment rights. And if you work for less than 8 hours, then you are not covered by this law. So make sure your contract states the number of hours you are employed to do.

If you are working term-time only, make sure that your contract states that you are continuously employed, so that the school holiday breaks do not count as a break in your employment contract. If they do, you will never build up the two years' employment in order to get protection under the EPCA.

You can get more detailed advice on hours and continuous employment from your trade union, local law centre or CAB. Other organisations that may help are New Ways to Work, Liberty (The National Council for Civil Liberties), the Women's Legal Defence Fund (WLDF) and The Maternity Alliance.

WHAT THE LAW SAYS

Equal opportunity policies and procedures have a basis in law – the Sex Discrimination Act, the Equal Pay Act and the Race Relations Act. These state that you must not be treated less favourably on the grounds of sex or of race in recruitment or selection, training, promotion, pay and other conditions of service.

Hopefully it won't be necessary for you to use the law to ensure fair treatment. But if you think you have been treated less favourably because you are a woman, or because you are a member of an ethnic minority group, you can make a complaint to an industrial tribunal. But get some advice first from the Equal Opportunities Commission, the Commission for Racial Equality, a law centre, the local community relations council, the Women's Legal Defence Fund or the National Council for Civil Liberties (Liberty). Go to one of these agencies as soon as possible after you think the discrimination has happened, because if you are thinking of taking legal action you must lodge your complaint with the industrial tribunal within three months of the act of discrimination.

EQUAL OPPORTUNITY STATEMENTS

As a result of equal opportunity policies, you may see statements in job adverts encouraging different groups of people to apply for the particular job. This encouragement is allowed by law, where those groups of people – women or black and ethnic minority people – have been under-represented in the particular area of work.

You may also receive an equal opportunity policy statement with the job application form and advice on how to complete the form.

MONITORING PROGRESS

Part of the application form may ask for information about your ethnic origin. You will be asked to place yourself in one of a number of categories which will include: white, black Afro-Caribbean, black British, Asian, and other. There may be other groups as well.

The Commission for Racial Equality (CRE) encourages

employers with equal opportunity policies to ask for this information. It is needed in order to monitor the effectiveness of the equal opportunity policy and to ensure that there is no discrimination, *not* to discriminate against you or in your favour. Quite often this part of the form is removed before the people doing the shortlisting see your application.

Some employers also like to monitor age, marital status, and gender, in order to ensure there is no bias in these respects in the selection procedure.

CONCLUSION

Getting a job can change your life – it can bring you financial independence, new interests and new friends. It can open new doors for you. Your job search may prove difficult – it may be time consuming and at times demoralising, but do not give up, because if you do get what you want, it will have been worth the battle.

FURTHER INFORMATION

USEFUL ADDRESSES

COMMISSION FOR RACIAL EQUALITY
Elliot House, 10/12 Allington Street, London SW1E 5EH
Tel: (071) 828 7022
EQUAL OPPORTUNITIES COMMISSION
Overseas House, Quay Street, Manchester M3 3HN
Tel: (061) 833 9244
LIBERTY (NATIONAL COUNCIL FOR CIVIL LIBERTIES)
21 Tabard Street, London SE1 4LA
Tel: (071) 403 3888

MATERNITY ALLIANCE
15 Britannia Street, London WC1X 9JP
Tel: (071) 837 1265
TRADES UNION CONGRESS (TUC)
Congress House, 23–28 Great Russell Street, London WC1B 3LS
Tel: (071) 636 4030
WOMEN'S LEGAL DEFENCE FUND
27 Great James Street, London WC1N 3BS

FOUR

STARTING A JOB

LESLEY HART

Lesley Hart MA, has 20 years' experience of working in education. For the past eight years she has been based in the Continuing Education Centre at the University of Strathclyde, where she has been responsible for running a wide range of women's courses. Having taken only a brief spell of maternity leave after the birth of her two children, she is well aware of the challenges facing a working mother. She is also co-author of a book entitled *Strategic Women*.

INTRODUCTION

Going back to paid work means the start of a very different way of life. Perhaps you will be returning to the same job that you did before your children were born, or perhaps you will be starting something new. Either way, you will be entering a different environment, establishing a new routine and perhaps making a totally new group of friends.

Returning to paid work as a mother means that you will have to juggle competing demands from dependants and employers. On the whole, paid work is not organised with parents' needs in mind. How many jobs are just for school hours? How many employers give time off when dependants are ill? You will have a disadvantage that many men do not – you will have to manage without a wife at home!

You may find that the workplace has changed too, many of the changes being technological. The introduction of facsimiles, computers, and word processors has led to new office systems and done away with a lot of paper work. There have also been changes in how work is organised. You may find that management styles have changed since you were last working, and some managers will try to involve you as much as possible in decisions about how things are done. You may find that your workplace offers a flexitime system, or has a bonus scheme, and you may find that your employer offers good opportunities for training.

This chapter looks at ways of coping with the return to work. It discusses how to survive those first few important weeks and suggests ways of overcoming the stress that you will inevitably feel as your time becomes more precious. Strategies are suggested for the management of your time so that the important domestic jobs get done and you still have some time for *you*. The chapter explores the changes in relationships that returning to work may bring and looks at how joining a network or support group has helped many women who have returned to work.

STARTING A JOB

The experience of starting a job is different for us all, but remember, everyone finds it takes a little while to settle into a new job. Experiences of women returners vary. Some find it quite straightforward:

> *I returned to work when my children were teenagers and I found it very positive. I enjoyed it, and the company was very encouraging. I didn't have any problems.*

Others find it more problematic.

> *I've just returned to work after having my second child and I've found that my experience has been that people tend to ignore the physical and emotional experience that I've had and just expect me to soldier on.*

Whether your first experiences are good or bad, there are bound to be times when you feel nervous and insecure –

everyone does. As we saw in chapter 1, being out of paid work saps self-confidence, partly at least, because we live in a society that values paid work above other things. Low self-confidence means that we devalue what we can do, we worry about fitting in and learning new skills, and we fear that we will fail.

When you start your new job remember to ask if you are unsure of anything, do not be hesitant about asking questions. Take time to find out exactly how things are done in the organisation where you are working. All organisations have different administrative systems which are often taken for granted and may not automatically be explained to new employees. This lack of communication is not a deliberate or conscious attempt to keep you in the dark, but is rather the result of employees following routines which are so obvious to them that they think that they are not worth mentioning. Asking questions as a new employee is expected and normal behaviour. If you have to absorb a great deal of new information in a short space of time do not trust your memory but, rather, write things down and keep the information in a safe place. Sometimes problems exist because organisations have introduced new equipment as Margaret, a 32-year-old secretary, found.

The first day when I returned to work was awful! Although I had been away for 18 months, the machine I had been using before had been updated with a memory bank and I could not work out exactly which buttons to press. I suffered a good deal of anxiety and stress that day, as I watched the wastebin filling up with more and more of my wasted efforts. I decided the next morning to take my time and find out exactly how the machine operated, even if this meant completing fewer assignments that day. By day three, I was feeling much more confident and was beginning to enjoy the work.

If you find yourself feeling unsettled or unhappy, try to raise issues that are bothering you with your manager, and/or discuss them with other people at the same level in your organisation. You could also share the experience with friends and family outside work as they could offer valuable support. Joining a trade union can also prove very helpful and supportive. You could also join a local Working Mother's Association where you will be able to discuss problems with others and can further increase your confidence (see end of chapter for details of UK Headquarters).

MAKING THE RIGHT IMPRESSION

Although employers are urging women to return to paid work, it is hard to judge just how sympathetic they are to working mothers' needs. Whether they show them or not, some men and women have less than positive attitudes towards working mothers. They may question your commitment to your job, and your reliability as an employee. So, it is crucial in your first weeks at work to try to make as good an impression as possible.

The first thing you should try to do is to build up good relationships with your work colleagues. This is an investment, because in the future, these are the people you are going to spend a major part of your day with. While you may lack some confidence at first, your experience as a mother should stand you in good stead. Developing new relationships with people requires a number of different skills, such as negotiating, problem solving and asserting yourself. These are skills which, whether you realise it or not, you will have developed when at home. Being a mother also develops your level of patience, tolerance and understanding; and these skills are extremely useful when working with other people.

If you are unlucky and have unsympathetic colleagues,

you may need to hide any problems that working may cause, as this woman returner found:

> I had young children and managed to return to work as one half of a job share, but within the first 24 hours I recognised that I was going to get a lot of opposition, particularly from the men I worked with. So, the idea of showing them that I had children, or any domestic problems, was impossible. I very quickly learnt to hide the fact that meetings in the evening were inconvenient and found that turning up late, or having any excuse that was related to my family, was bad news.

You also need to try and make sure that your childcare arrangements are 'bomb-proof', at least initially.

Coping with children's illnesses is a problem that women returners all have to deal with at some time. In many other European countries parents can take time off when their children are ill, but in Britain no such leave arrangement currently exists. In Britain, therefore, mothers need to judge, on an individual basis, how open they can be with their employer about taking leave in times of crisis. Lindsay, a 33-year-old returner, found that she had a fairly understanding employer:

> I had been back at work six months when my six-year-old caught chicken-pox. I really didn't know what to say to my employer, but decided that honesty was the best policy. He was, I am glad to say, relatively understanding and agreed that I could take a mixture of paid and unpaid leave for one week. After that, my mother came to stay to help with Colin's convalescence and I could return to work. In my three years back at work, this is the only major block of time I ever had to ask for. If, occasionally, a crisis occurs, I have come in

> *late or left early and made up the time. Everything's*
> *worked out okay for me, but I do have one or two*
> *friends who find that they can't be as honest and end*
> *up phoning in sick themselves if their children are ill.*

While trying hard to make a good impression, it is important not to go too far. Just as children and parents do not like change, work colleagues probably won't appreciate immediate suggestions about change either. Coming in as an outsider, you may well see all kinds of improvements that could be made. Unless you are in a very senior position, you are probably better off keeping your suggestions to yourself. Your suggestions will also be listened to much more seriously once you are an established member of the company.

COPING WITH STRESS

It is likely that you will, at some stage, feel stressed and under pressure when you first return to work. If and when this happens, try to make some time available for yourself and implement a personally devised strategy that you know helps to relieve your tension. Some women go hill-walking, some take a bath, some play sport. Many phone a friend for a chat and find that being able to talk about problems and stressful situations really helps.

It is also good for you to continue with leisure time interests, although you have to be realistic and look carefully at the amount of time at present allocated to this part of your life. The ideal is to get a good balance. If you are involved in a job where you are sitting behind a desk all day, it is sensible, refreshing and good for you to take some exercise when you come home after work. If, on the other hand, your job entails standing on your feet all day, a more relaxing leisure time interest might be the best thing for you. Always remember that stress and pressure are part of everyone's life. Feeling stressed is not a problem in itself but knowing how to cope with it can be.

BALANCING THE DEMANDS OF HOME AND WORK

A problem for many mothers, and particularly those with paid jobs, is time. You will need, as far as possible, to try and *manage* your time. This means deciding on priorities and planning ahead so that you live in some kind of order and still find time for things that you want to do, as well as coping with the things you need to do. There are a number of areas where you can rationalise your work, either by doing less of it or getting someone else to do it. One of these areas is housework. Housework is likely to be one of those chores which is a considerable drain on your time, and one that you could try to cut down. There are a number of options that you could consider:

1 Do the same amount of housework and probably sleep less (not a strategy to be developed in any long-term scale).
2 Pay someone else to do the housework.
3 Buy labour-saving devices which will cut down the amount of time spent on housework.
4 Negotiate with your family about sharing household duties.
5 Just do less housework!

Options 2 and 3 may be possible if you have the money to spare. Option 3 may not reduce the amount of work you do significantly and you may not approve of someone else doing your housework. Option 4 is a good long-term plan if your partner or children are able to help, but it may be a difficult plan to introduce immediately, especially if your partner and/or children have been used to you being responsible for all household tasks. Do not feel guilty, certainly in the short term, about option 5 – your house will not fall down just because some extra dust accumulates!

You should consider developing one or more or perhaps a mixture of the above strategies, depending on your own personal and economic standpoints.

Whatever you do, however, do not try to be superwoman. It is much better to work out compromises that are acceptable to both yourself and your family than to over-work. A good exercise to undertake is to write down a list of all household duties undertaken by you each week with the time allocation for each duty. Is it *all* essential? Which tasks can only be done by you and which tasks could be undertaken by somebody else? Which tasks could be done less often? Try to spread the load somehow so that you do not become over-burdened, over-tired and over-worked!

For most women, planning time is difficult due to the number of external influences on their lives. One cannot plan, for example, that your son will fall off his bike next Thursday and timetable for a visit to the hospital. Nor do you know in advance when the washing machine will break down, or the cat needs taking to the vet, or when a rush job at work will require you to work late. Neat timetables look great in theory, but do not always work in practice. Returning to work certainly means being organised and will involve a certain amount of planning. You should, however, recognise the need for flexibility and should not rely totally on a timetable of events! There is a good deal of evidence to show that women are very good at multi-tasking (doing several things at once). They are good at this both in the home and at work, and most women cope admirably with the many and varied demands on their time. Use the prepared timetable at the end

of this chapter to help you plan your time.

Patricia, a 35-year-old woman returner with three children aged 10, 8 and 6, describes how she manages her time.

> I went back to work last year when my youngest went to school. I certainly am more organised, and plan more carefully since I started work. I am not, however, fanatical like some of my working friends are about timetables, rotas etc. I like to spend some time on a Sunday evening working out the main priorities for the week. All the family are involved in this which I think is crucial. But what works for my family will not necessarily work for somebody else's household. It is really a matter of finding out what suits you and your family, and what is practical to achieve given time constraints.

Even when you're not working, life can seem like a race against time and certainly there is unlikely to be any gap in a woman's day when she just sits still, twiddles her thumbs and contemplates the ways of the world. So when you return to work you have to accept that certain things in your life may have to change.

CHANGES TO RELATIONSHIPS

Relationships with everyone will probably change when you return to work. You will have to cope with people's attitudes towards you changing and you may well feel you need support in order to cope.

RELATIONSHIPS WITH YOUR CHILDREN

Going back to work will almost definitely alter your relationships with your children. Most working mothers, however, claim that as well as changing the relationship, it improves it. One woman returner found that the only time she had problems with her children was when she briefly stopped work through being made redundant:

> I had been back at work two years when I was made redundant and did not work for two months. My children didn't like me being back in the house all day. I hadn't realised how independent they had become and their daily routines were quite firmly set. The whole family was delighted when I found alternative work!

Children no longer take it for granted that you will be there at their beck and call and most learn to respect and value you more. Children are creatures of habit. You must remember that they are used to having you there all the time and it may take a bit of negotiating to get them into a new routine. Fortunately, most children accept new routines quite quickly and you should be able to leave your house for work knowing that your children are still being properly cared for and looked after. It is essential that childcare arrangements are thought about carefully and depending on the age of your children, discussed with them as well. Many friends and relatives will give you advice about childcare, but what is really important is that the childcare arrangements made are ones that suit you and ones that you feel happy and relaxed with. Do not be pressurised into any childcare arrangements with which you are not happy.

IF YOU HAVE A PARTNER

Your relationship with your partner will also be different when you return to work. It is difficult to generalise about a partner's attitudes, but listed below are some quotes from women who attended a return to work course and comments taken from questionnaires they completed after being in work for six months.

My husband has been totally supportive and a great practical help in the house.

Returning to work has definitely improved my husband's relationship with the children. He now returns home earlier than he used to and spends more time with them.

My partner is a great moral support, but gives no great practical help to me. It is very much his view that I can and should return to work, but that it shouldn't affect his lifestyle!

> *My entering an all-male workforce worried my*
> *husband to begin with. I seemed to spend my time*
> *talking about my male colleagues and this probably*
> *made things worse. He now accepts the situation,*
> *although I think he would prefer me to work in an*
> *organisation more equally balanced with males and*
> *females.*

As you can see, the attitudes of partners vary and it is important that you talk to your partner fully about the implications of your returning to work. Possible minor problems not sorted out before you return can multiply into major difficulties once in work.

PARENTS AND RELATIVES

Most children adapt quickly to changes in their lives. But, this may not be so true of other people in your life. Your own parents and in-laws and other relatives may wonder at, and/or openly criticise their daughters or daughters-in-law returning to work and will voice many reservations about how their son/son-in-law and children could be properly looked after by a working mother. Many women feel that it is easier to explain their return to work to their children than to their parents. Again it is often a question of change of routine. Parents may be used to their daughters or daughters-in-law telephoning each day or visiting, and returning to work can seem to some of them like being abandoned. The criticisms that some openly voice about women deserting their children often overlay a fear that they themselves are being deserted. It is important, therefore, that contact is kept up, especially in the initial period of returning to work, so that parents do not feel left out.

Marie, a 28-year-old woman returner with one child aged

4, found, for example, that problems with her mother have eventually been solved.

> *I returned to work, partly for economic and partly for social reasons, when my daughter was just two years old. My mother was initially shocked and disappointed. She felt that her grandchild could not possibly be looked after properly by someone else and that I was being selfish and unthinking. Two years on, when she sees that she has a well-balanced, normal granddaughter and sees that her daughter is doing well at work, she has changed her mind and now boasts on my successes to her friends.*

FRIENDS

Relationships with friends can vary enormously; some will support you, some will be envious of you, some will be critical of you. Remember that keeping up friendships takes time and effort and that it is easy to lose contact with friends once you return to work. It is well worthwhile making a positive effort to remain in contact with your friends. You will also find that going back to work will involve you in making new friends and this, in fact, can be a great pleasure as Margaret, a 39-year-old returner, found.

> *Before I returned to work my friends all seemed to be people of my own age and looking back, our conversations always seemed fairly narrow and introspective. I have really enjoyed making new friends, especially meeting and talking with some of the younger people at work – I had forgotten all about the excitement of planning weekends and meetings with boyfriends! I have also made a number of good friends amongst older people at work and they have been a great help and support to me.*

NETWORKS AND SUPPORT MEETINGS

Most problems and challenges that you will face when you return to work will be ones already faced by previous women returners. In order to exchange experiences, swop information and help with career development, a number of women's networks and support groups have been established all over the UK. Joining a network can prove very positive and useful, and some examples of existing networks are included at the end of this chapter. Elizabeth, a 33-year-old woman returner, describes how joining her local network helped her.

> *I found the first three months of working really stressful. I was the only woman returner in my section of what was quite a large organisation. Nobody seemed to bother much about me and certainly there were no concessions made with regard to my domestic commitments. I had nobody therefore at work with whom I could discuss my problems and I found that at home my partner and my children weren't particularly sympathetic or understanding either. By joining my local Network, I have met lots of other women who I find are in exactly the same position as myself. Just talking about problems seems almost to solve them.*

If no formal networks exist in your area, meeting informally with friends and colleagues can be equally useful, or you could always consider starting a network yourself.

CONCLUSION

So, what have most women found about going back to work? You will be glad to know that women who are followed up after Return to Work courses mainly say that they find it easier than they thought they would. They enjoy their work, they are happy in it and many of the hurdles that they thought they would encounter have not materialised. Being prepared, being organised, being committed and enthusiastic are all elements that go together to ensure that your return to work is a successful one.

FURTHER INFORMATION

USEFUL ADDRESSES

THE PARENT NETWORK
44–46 Caversham Road, London NW5 2DS
Tel: (071) 485 8535
WOMEN RETURNERS' NETWORK (WRN)
Euston House, 81–103 Euston Street, London NW1 2ET
Contact: Ruth Michael (Chair)
Tel: (071) 388 3111
THE WORKING MOTHERS' ASSOCIATION
77 Holloway Road, London N7 8JZ
Tel: (071) 700 5771

NOTES ON THE GROUPS

THE PARENT NETWORK
This group is run by parents, for parents to enable them to meet and share the experiences and challenges of family life.

WOMEN RETURNERS' NETWORK
This network promotes women's re-entry into the labour force through education, training and employment opportunities. It provides useful information to employers and encourages tutors, trainers and course developers to provide flexible programmes.

THE WORKING MOTHERS' ASSOCIATION
This is a network of support groups of working parents which provides an opportunity to exchange information and experience.

USEFUL BOOKS

- *How to Survive as a Working Mother,* Judith M Steiner, Kogan Page, 1989
- *Returning to Work – A Practical Guide for Women,* Alec Reed, Kogan Page, 1989
- *Women Can Achieve Career Success,* Maggie Steel & Zita Thornton, Grapevine, 1988
- *Women Can Return to Work,* Maggie Steel & Zita Thornton, Grapevine, 1988

WEEKLY TIME-PLAN CHART

Completing a time-plan chart can help you to see how you allocate your time at present. It can also be useful when planning future use of time. There is an example of one on the next page.

	7-9 am	9-11 am	11 am-1 pm	1-3 pm	3-5 pm	5-7 pm	7-9 pm	9-11 pm
Mon								
Tues								
Wed								
Thur								
Fri								
Sat								
Sun								

CHAPTER

FIVE

CHILDCARE

CAROLINE BAMFORD

Caroline Bamford lives in Scotland where she works as a freelance writer and researcher.

She has researched, taught and written on women's issues since 1977 when she began her doctorate. Since its completion she has worked as a researcher for Strathclyde University and as an Education Officer for BBC Education. She combined a job share at the BBC with teaching and research in Women's Studies. Caroline left the BBC post in 1990 and now combines writing and research with caring for her two-year-old daughter. She has recently published *Gender and Education in Scotland – A Review of Research* (SIACE, Edinburgh 1988).

INTRODUCTION

In Britain, most women leave their jobs after having a baby. Only two or three women in ten return to work after taking maternity leave: the rest leave, perhaps planning to return once their children are 'on their feet', or have started school, or have left home. Perhaps, also, they leave because they have no real sense, in those intense first months after the birth, of the shape their lives will take in the future. In most European countries, more women return than in Britain. Only the Netherlands has a lower rate: one out of ten, while in Sweden, Germany and Denmark, the figure is eight out of ten.

One reason why these differences are so great is that almost half of the women at work in Britain do not qualify for statutory maternity leave. Another is because some countries have places in publicly funded nurseries for most pre-school children, whereas others, such as Britain, have places for very few. This means that women in Britain have to rely on private arrangements for the care of their children while they are at work, with all that that implies. Most women in Britain have to compromise: they simply cannot find or afford the childcare that they would like. Many return to work part-time – in fact, the UK has the highest proportion of part-time workers in Europe. And they opt for whatever childcare is available and what they can afford, often supplementing this with a number of other arrangements to cover the hours that they have to work.

Research shows that lack of childcare is stopping many women from returning to work. Gallup conducted a survey of women who are not in paid employment and who have children to care for. Almost two-thirds of the women they interviewed said that they would like to return to paid work. More than three-quarters of these – 79 per cent – said that they were prevented from returning by having young children to look after. A third of the women with school-age children in the sample said that they would return immediately if adequate childcare arrangements could be made. (See *School's Out*, Winter 1989/90, p. 16.) So childcare clearly has a central role in determining whether women feel able to return to work.

Mothers are trapped not only by lack of childcare but also by beliefs about what it means to be a good mother. We live in a society which believes that mothers should put their children first and that the best way to do this is to be with them all day at home. A survey carried out by the Government in 1981 – the *Women and Employment* survey – found that 80 per cent of the men and women who were interviewed believed that a married woman with a pre-school child should either stay at home or go out to work only if she 'really needs the money'. (See J. Martin and C. Roberts, *Women and Employment: A Lifetime Perspective* (1984), HMSO.) It is no accident that there is so little publicly funded childcare in the UK – this has also been the view that successive Governments have held.

These ideas are starting to change. But while employers and others are beginning to acknowledge the skills and qualities that women who are mothers can bring to the workplace, few people are drawing attention to the benefits (other than money) that being an employed mother can bring to children, partners and relatives at home. So mothers are left to weigh up the options for themselves, often with little practical help and emotional support and with an underlying worry that perhaps it would be better for her children if she stayed at home.

Britain, it seems, is slow to challenge the belief that young children need their mothers full-time. In their book *New Mothers at Work*, Julia Brannen and Peter Moss found that:

> *In Sweden, Denmark, France and Belgium, for instance, there is now widespread acceptance of women working when they have young children, and of the idea that even very young children can benefit from the experience of shared care, whether or not their parents work.*

In the USA, the question of whether children are adversely affected from their mothers going out to work is not a subject of debate: it is accepted that they do not suffer at all.

In Britain, the belief that a good mother is at home for and with her children places additional pressures on women returning to paid employment. They have to try to satisfy themselves that the childcare arrangements they have made are good for their children; that they are not letting their children down by working. They may also have to cope with negative attitudes from employers, colleagues, relatives, possibly even from the person who is looking after their child while they are at work.

Recent research into childcare for young children should

put mothers' minds at rest. The evidence, to quote from Marion Kozak in *Daycare for Kids*, is that 'as long as the care is consistent, dependable and of high quality, it is agreed that babies and toddlers develop equally well in non-maternal and maternal care'. (Daycare Trust, p. 10.) For school-age children the key seems to be finding a carer and an environment that they enjoy and that gives them space to choose their own activities. In this chapter, we will look at different kinds of childcare and how to find out what is available. We will also look at how to judge whether a particular person or place is a good choice for your child and make suggestions for things that you could do to help your arrangements work well.

This chapter has been written with the assumption that most people looking after children are women. However, in practice, some childcarers are men. Many grandfathers look after grandchildren and some nursery staff and childminders are men too. Some nurseries try hard to recruit men so that children can develop caring relationships with both men and women and this may be particularly valuable if a child is cared for by a single parent at home.

PRE-SCHOOL CARE

If you are planning to return to work and have a young child, there are several different kinds of childcare for you to consider. What is available to you, and how much it will cost, varies from area to area, and it will probably take you some time to find out about it and to make an arrangement that suits you and your child or children. In practice, most women know the kind of care that they would like and stop their search if they find someone or somewhere that fits roughly with this. But it is worthwhile to search more widely if you have the time before returning to work. You may find something that you like more, or your first arrangement may fall through, or the child may not settle in the place you choose and you will need an alternative arrangement to fall back on.

RELATIVES

Some women have a close relative who is able to look after their children. In fact, having a mother or mother-in-law who is willing to provide childcare can make having a baby and returning to work seem possible for some women. The advantages are that you do not have to search out options and you can avoid having to take the risk of leaving your child with someone who is almost a stranger.

But before you commit yourself to this kind of care, it would be wise to consider the factors that make other forms of childcare work well. Do you have a good relationship with your relative? Are you able to talk openly with her about your child and his or her needs? Do you broadly agree on important issues, such as discipline, food, crying, sleeping? If not, do you think your relative will do things your way? Is your relative's house a safe place for a small child to be? Will your child be taken out? Will he or she see other children?

You will also have to decide between you what you are going to pay, what the hours will be and what you will do about holidays. So it would be useful for you to look at the sections in this chapter on childminders and nannies where carers' pay and conditions are described so that you are in a better position to discuss your needs with your relative. This may help you to avoid disagreements or misunderstandings in the future. This is one mother's experience:

> I have a good relationship with my mother and she has been very supportive of the way that I have wanted to bring up children. So I always knew I wouldn't have a

> problem in asking her to look after my son in a
> particular way. For me the real benefit of having
> relatives look after Jamie is that there is much more
> flexibility than there often is with a childminder. For
> example, if I get home late from work, my Mum is
> happy to keep him and give him his tea. I can see that it
> could be more difficult to have a child looked after by a
> relative you know less well such as a mother-in-law
> where it might be difficult to resolve any conflicts.

In fact, there does seem to be greater chance of tensions and
disagreements developing if the mother-in-law, rather than
the mother, does the childcare.

CHILDMINDERS

Many women returners leave their pre-school children with
a childminder – with someone who looks after other people's
children in his or her home. By law, anyone who looks after a
child or children under 5 (and from October 1991, under 8
years) in his or her own home for two or more hours a day, for
pay, is required to register. Only if the child is a close relative
of the carer – such as a grandchild – is registration
unnecessary. This means that your local social services
department (or, in Strathclyde, your education department)
will have a list of registered childminders, and it may also
know who has vacancies for a child of your child's age.

The registration of childminders does give you some safe-
guards. Local authorities vary in the kinds of registration
procedures they use. But as a minimum they will have
checked that neither the minder nor other adults in the
household have a record of offences against children or have
had their own children taken into local authority care. They
will check that the minder is reasonably healthy and they
will visit his or her home and check that it is suitable – that

there are guards on the fires, that there is enough space etc. Once registered, he or she should be regularly visited by someone from the local authority. Some social services are very thorough in their enquiries, taking up references from health visitors, housing departments, doctors and even the police. Some also require that potential minders attend a training day. Because these checks vary, you may like to ask your own social services department about the procedure that they have used to register childminders.

There are also guidelines about how many children a childminder can look after at one time. While these numbers vary slightly between authorities, the maximum allowed is usually three children under 5 years, only one of whom may be under one year old. This maximum includes the minder's own children.

While local authorities register childminders, they do not set their rates of pay. Childminders are self-employed and responsible for their own tax and national insurance payments. How much they charge varies a great deal from area to area. Each year, the National Childminding Association issues guidelines on childminders' pay and conditions, basing these on an annual survey of the charges that its members make. The range of charges reported in January 1990 was £30 to £75 per week, and 80p to £2.75 per hour. They recommended, for 1990, a minimum weekly rate of £45 per child; a minimum daily rate of £9; and a minimum hourly rate of £1.10.

You may find that there are no vacancies for registered childminders in your area. It is estimated that there are ten times as many unregistered childminders as registered ones, so you could still find someone to meet your needs. Some local authorities are very slow to process registrations, so quite a few of these women could be waiting for theirs to be processed. If you do not find someone who is already working as a childminder you may have to find your own.

How do you find a suitable childminder? First of all, you should contact your local Social Services department. If you are lucky, they will know which childminders have vacancies and will be able to give you a list of childminders who live near you or your place of work. You could advertise in your local newspaper or on newsagents' cards, or you may hear from a friend of someone who is interested. The National Childminding Association may be able to help too. They have produced several booklets, including *A Parents' Guide to Childminding*, and may be able to give you a contact number for a local childminders' group.

Once you have identified possible childminders, you will have to decide whether they can meet your and your child's needs. Even if someone is registered, it doesn't mean that they are good at their job. While local authority checks may include whether an applicant has relevant training and experience, they are not designed to assess the caring skills of potential minders. This is something you will have to do for yourself. So you will have to visit possible childminders and interview people who are not working as childminders but who you think might be suitable until you find someone, and somewhere, that you feel happy with. When you are doing this, you might find it helpful to keep the following checklist in mind:

- Is the minder a mother herself?
- Are her children jealous of other children being looked after in the house? How does she handle this?
- Does she have any kind of training? (She may, for example, have taken a nursery nurse course, or nurse's training, or teacher training before her own children were born.)
- Is the house geared towards children? Is the house reasonably safe and clean?
- Are there plenty of toys within the children's reach?

- Does she have a garden where the children can play?
- What kind of things does she do with the children all day? Does she organise the children around her own house-work, or does she put the children first?
- Does she care for the children, or does she simply mind them? Does she pay the children attention, cuddle them, play with them?
- How does she discipline the childen? (It is illegal for a childminder to smack a child.)
- How many children does she look after? How many more would she like to take on?
- What kind of food does she give the children? (Most childminders provide children's meals, although you could suggest taking food for your child with you.) You should also ask whether there is any extra charge for food.
- Does she, or do other people in the household, smoke?
- Are there any pets in the house? Are they kept under control?
- What hours can you leave your child for? Is there enough flexibility to cover your being late when dropping-off or collecting your child?
- Do other parents keep their children away if they are ill?
- Does the minder have any back-up if she is ill? (If she is a registered childminder, the social services department will, wherever possible, arrange cover for her, or she may have a friend or relative who she would ask to help out.)
- What is her rate of pay? What does she charge for holidays and sickness?
- Does she charge an overtime rate and extra for outings?
- Would you need to pay a retainer to secure a place?
- Is she insured?
- Does she take the children out by car? If so, are car safety seats/seat belts fitted?

If you find that she would like to look after your child, that the hours and the place and the pay all suit you, you will probably decide on how you feel about the woman herself. It is important that you choose someone you feel you can trust and who has a good rapport with children. You will also feel more comfortable if it is someone you get on with. It is much easier to leave your child with someone you like. This also makes it much easier to discuss what kind of day she and the children have had and how your child is getting on.

It is also wise to draw up some kind of contract with your childminder, putting down on paper her rate of pay, hours, and any special arrangements so that you both know where you stand. She will also need a note of how to contact you in an emergency and the name and address of your doctor.

While childminding still gets a bad press, it can be a very good form of childcare. If you and your child 'click' with the minder, then you will have another person in your life who knows and cares for your child, who can discuss how he or she is getting on, and who can make suggestions about how to keep him or her happy. When my baby was small, I loved having another woman who I could discuss her with: she was reassuring, helpful and supportive. This was Jan's experience too:

> I've learned from Veronica some of the ideas I now use habitually in looking after Islay. I would see her doing something and think, 'of course, that's how it should be done'. I don't have relatives locally who might have played such a role. Because Veronica was confident with Islay, she would talk to me about what had happened during the day. We talked about my experiences with the baby, comparing Islay with her own daughters. I definitely gained confidence from finding another woman who wasn't worried about 'controlling' babies and who saw it as normal to worry about why they were crying!

In their book *New Mothers at Work* Julia Brannan and Peter Moss found that women who chose relatives or childminders to look after their children often did so because they wanted their child to have a close, one-to-one relationship with the caregiver. They also found that many women who would not choose childminding as their 'ideal' form of care came to value it over time.

Even if you feel that on the whole the relationship between the carer and your child is working out quite well, you probably will disagree about something. Another finding in Julia Brennan and Peter Moss's study was that more than half of the women they interviewed reported at least one instance where they disagreed with the child's carer. Food was the main source of disagreement. Mothers felt that carers gave their children too many sticky cakes and sweets and undermined their attempts to establish a healthy diet. The other main area of disagreement is physical care and safety, for example not changing nappies enough, or leaving children out in the cold.

Many of these mothers did not raise these disagreements with the carer. They did not want to hurt their feelings, or they thought it might makes things worse. But they also felt that they would like to be able to talk more openly with their carer, not just about disagreements, but also about more general things such as how their child had spent his or her day. These mothers' experiences underline the importance of trying to choose a minder whom you feel you can talk to. You will also need to find time to talk, perhaps by setting up a routine of always talking about the child's day when you go and pick him or her up.

You may be unlucky though and find that the childminder you have chosen is not working out for you or your child. If you met no one else who would be suitable when you were first looking and if there are no childminders who you like with vacancies, you may decide to try recruiting your own.

Jan, who came to value her childminder so much, had recruited her herself:

Having tried to find a childminder through the social services department and having had an unhappy experience with a registered childminder, I decided to advertise for someone who could come to our house and mind the baby at home. I wanted to encourage applicants who would take an active role in caring for my child, rather than the more passive role implied by the term 'minder'. I was also able to pay more than the going rate for childminding. The wording of the ad had to be puzzled over. In the end I settled for something like 'responsible person required to help care for six-month-old girl'. There were three responses. None of them wanted to come to us, although the person I chose was willing to try it. She came to our house for an informal interview. I was impressed because she could articulate her ideas about childcare, she had a sense of humour and was willing to work with me over caring for Islay. She'd also brought up two girls of her own and had cared for a handicapped child. She was confident and at the same time sensitive in playing with Islay. She said that she would prefer to look after Islay in her home, and we agreed to give it a try. We spent the next day together – partly in the car and partly in my work-place. I saw how clever Veronica was at diverting Islay from crying and that was it. Veronica took Islay to her house the next day and somehow it fell into place very smoothly. She has now registered as a childminder and looks after two other children as well.

In addition to advertising locally, you could try asking around. Friends, and friends' childminders, may know of someone who is thinking of becoming a childminder. With someone who is just starting as a childminder, you may also be in a better position to negotiate the kinds of hours and the kind of care that you would like. If you do find someone this way, you could recommend to her that, in addition to registering, she joins the National Childminding Association. They should have local members who will know the ropes in her area, and they will be able to offer practical help and advice.

NANNIES: CARERS WHO COME TO YOU

The word nanny conjures up a stereotype that is very far from typical these days. The matron in uniform who lives-in is only a tiny minority of the women who look after children in their parent's homes. Nannies, in this much broader sense, include women who have taken a training course, women with practical experience but no training, and women who have retired and find that they have time on their hands. Most of them have their own homes to go back to at night. In fact, many women who employ carers in their homes call them childminders, not nannies, perhaps because they feel uncomfortable with what the word 'nanny' conjures up. In this section we will look at how to decide whether having someone come to you is the best option, and if so, how to recruit someone you feel you can trust.

The first consideration for many women will be cost. If a nanny is only going to be caring for your child or children then she will only have what you pay her to live on. If you have a partner who is earning, you could consider childcare to be a joint cost, and take his or her earnings into account when working out what you can afford. But most women do not do this – they feel that they have to be able to pay childcare costs out of the money that *they* earn. According to

the latest edition of the *Working Mother's Handbook*, published in June 1989, the 'going rate' for a daily nanny is
£2.50–£3.50 per hour, i.e. £100–£160 per week. For a live-in
nanny, the rate is £60–£80, but you will also have to provide
accommodation and meals. You should also pay her national
insurance contributions and income tax. While this may
seem a lot out of your wages, you may find, if you have more
than one child, that the cost of employing a nanny is not that
much more than the cost of using a nursery.

The second consideration is whether you would prefer to
have someone to come to you, rather than taking your children to them. This does have definite advantages. You will
have someone on hand to look after your children when they
are ill and you might have more control over how she cares
for your child or children than you would have with a
childminder or nursery. It is a more flexible arrangement too
– you may not be tied to fixed or regular hours of childcare.
She would also be able to give your child more individual
attention than a childminder or nursery might be able to do.
You will also have to be prepared for someone coming into
your life more than a childminder would because she is in
your home all day.

There are disadvantages too. Younger women who work
as nannies tend to change jobs quite often. Your children
may not have very regular contact with others. You will need
to leave your house reasonably tidy for her. She will probably invite her friends, who are nannies, round. You may feel
that she needs some supervision. She may fall ill or be
unpunctual. And you will be directly responsible for
employing someone, with all that that involves.

If you *do* decide that a nanny is the best kind of care for
you, how do you go about recruiting someone suitable? In
her book *Good Working Mother's Guide*, Mary Beard gives
detailed advice about employing a nanny, from deciding the
kind of person you would like, to completing tax returns.

She emphasises the importance of working out your needs, the kind of employment that you can offer and the *style* of nanny that would suit you best before you advertise. She recommends that you decide whether you want someone to live in or live out; whether there are groups of people who you would exclude, such as smokers or people who do not drive; whether you want someone who would also do some domestic work; what kind of personal qualities you would like the person to have; and of course, what you can afford to pay. In addition, you will need to weigh up the advantages of experience and training, experience looking after her own children as well as other people's.

What kinds of course might a nanny have taken? Most trained nannies will have followed a National Nursery Examination Board course or the Scottish equivalent, the SCOTVEC National Certificate in Nursery Nursing. This is a two-year course covering all aspects of the care of children from birth to the age of 7. A typical course includes three days a week at college and two days gaining practical experience in a maternity unit, a nursery class, a school, or a private family. There are also some private colleges that offer specialised training, preparing young women to be today's version of the traditional nanny of old. Fees are high, so these women will probably come from families with some money behind them. Their training is similar – they also take the NNEB certificate – and they get practical experience at the college nursery. There are some other courses that nannies might have taken, for example the National Association of Maternal and Child Welfare courses that some students take at school.

Not all women who respond to an advert for a nanny will have taken a course, and it is up to you to decide how important you think training is. The Working Mother's Association guide, *The Working Mother's Handbook*, concludes that:

> In our experience, the nanny's personality counts as much as her training. Although the training includes much which is very valuable – child development, the importance of play, some medical knowledge – many girls may still be inexperienced in looking after one or two children in the home, unsupervised . . . Perhaps the most crucial issue is that you feel you can get on well together and trust each other.
>
> (p. 15)

Once you have worked out your needs and preferences, it is time to start your search. You may find someone through word of mouth (perhaps by mentioning that you are looking for a nanny to a friend who already has one who will pass the information on). You may find someone by advertising in your local paper or, especially if you live in London, in the *Lady* and *Nursery World*. You may also find someone through a licensed nanny/mother's agency.

When you advertise, it is wise to be quite precise so that you do not have to disappoint too many applicants. This is the wording that Fiona used:

> Nanny for new born baby. Forty hours per week from mid-April. Edinburgh, Marchmont area, live-out. Experience/NNEB preferred. Good wage for right person. Please apply in writing.

Once you have drawn up a shortlist, you will need to interview possible candidates. You might find it best to hold two interviews, the first to find out who would be suitable, and the second with just two or three candidates. This would give you a chance to get to know each other better and for the candidates to spend some time with your child or children before you make your final choice.

Here are some of the things that Mary Beard in *Good*

Working Mother's Guide suggests you cover when you interview candidates:

1 Ask her about her last job – what she liked and disliked; how long she stayed and why she is leaving. If she has only just qualified then ask her about her college course.
2 Ask her what she would do from day to day, and what she *does* do from day to day in her present job.
3 Ask her how long she would intend to stay in the job.
4 Discuss your approach to childcare – to things like sweets, television, punishment, to 'boys' and 'girl's' games.
5 Ask her how she would deal with difficult situations, such as your child having a tantrum.
6 Check carefully that she meets the terms of your advert – e.g. that she is a non-smoker.
7 Make sure she knows the hours, the holiday entitlement, and the pay (before or after deductions for tax and national insurance).
8 Ask about her references – whom to contact, and whether to contact her present employer.
9 If she is going to live-in, then show her the room and clarify things like whether she will eat with you all the time, and how you feel about guests staying overnight.

You will need, at some stage, to take up references. Some applicants will have brought references with them, but you would be well advised to check these by phoning the referee up. Mary Beard suggests that these are the kinds of things you ask the referee:

1 What are the nanny's best qualities? What failings did they feel she had?
2 What kinds of things did she do with the children?
3 Would the referee positively recommend the nanny for your job?

Mary Beard also suggests that you ask about her record for illness, why she left or is leaving, and any reservations the referee might have.

Once you have chosen someone, you will need to draw up a contract of employment, and, once she has accepted this, let the unsuccessful applicants know. The contract should specify terms and conditions like hours, pay, holidays and duties. It is important to stick to the conditions that you agree. Many nannies decide to leave because their employers start to expect more from them, for example by increasing their hours or adding to their duties. This is how Fiona set about being a good employer:

> Once Rob and I decided that we would like to employ a nanny, we realised we knew very little about how to go about it. We spoke to our friends to find out about rates of pay, and found that it is a very mixed up business. We wanted to do it right – to make the right deductions for tax and National Insurance and still leave the nanny with a decent take home wage. In the end we agreed on £100 per week take-home pay for a 40-hour week with a pay rise every year. We wanted her to have the kinds of conditions of employment that other people have, so we drew up a contract and laid down guidelines for the things we expected her to do. We also agreed that every three months we would sit down formally to discuss how things were going.

Once you have found and employed someone, you will have to try and make sure that the arrangement works well. Like Fiona, you may decide to have regular formal discussions, as well as more frequent informal chats about how she and your child are getting on. If you see that your child is settled and happy, you should come to trust your nanny and let her take charge. This was Diana's experience:

> I found I needed to strike a balance between setting
> ground rules, for things that I saw as very important,
> and not being too controlling. I didn't want to smother
> my nanny's freedom of movement or initiative as I
> knew that she would enjoy her job more, and do it
> better, if I let her do things in her own way. I grew to
> trust her completely so that while she did do some
> things I disagreed with, these ceased to really matter.

For many women, the cost of employing a nanny, and the
disadvantage of your child having little regular contact with
other children, makes nanny sharing an attractive option. Of
course, you still have to find someone to share with. It is
most likely to work out if you can find someone who you like
and can talk to, so that you can openly review how things are
going every once in a while. You will also need to think
ahead to future needs, and try to work out whether the
arrangement is likely to work as the children get older and
their needs change. Here are the kinds of practical arrangements that the *Working Mother's Handbook* suggests that
you work out in advance:

● Whose house will the children be in?
● Will the nanny be able to cope with the changing needs of
  children of different ages?
● What equipment will the nanny need – a double buggy?
  Two high chairs?
● Do you have similar ideas about childcare, about issues
  such as food, play, outings, and dealing with problems
  such as bullying or jealousy?
● What will you do if one of the children is ill?
● What will you do about holidays? Will you take them at
  the same time?
● What would you do if a new baby came on to the scene?
● How will plans for nursery and primary school fit in with

the arrangement? (*The Working Mother's Association,* 1990, pp. 18–19.)

If you *do* find someone to share with (perhaps by advertising in your local *National Childbirth Trust* newsletter), if you find a nanny who you both like, and if you can sort out all the practical details, then you have an arrangement that can work well. I found that my one-year-old loved going to the house of a three-year-old to be looked after by her nanny. Perhaps it is the youngest child who benefits most, but Alice remained devoted to her older playmate through thick and thin.

NURSERIES

There are several different kinds of nurseries in the UK which together care for just under 2 per cent of under-fives. All nurseries have to be registered and must comply with strict regulations governing the ratio of staff to children, the minimum childcare qualifications that staff must have, and safety and planning matters. As with registered childminders, your local social services department (or education department in Strathclyde) will be able to give a list of nurseries in your area. What kinds of nurseries are there?

Local authority day nurseries are run by local authorities. In most areas, spaces are very limited and are reserved for parents and children who are in greatest need. Children are usually given priority if they are considered to be 'at risk', and possibly because they come from single-parent households, or low-income households, or live in areas of deprivation. Some authorities – Manchester, Sheffield, Strathclyde, and some boroughs in London – are changing their policies so that all local children could qualify for a place. But places are scarce, so if you want nursery provision for your child you will probably have to look elsewhere.

Voluntary or community nurseries have usually been set
up by a group of local parents and are open to all. They usually receive some subsidy from the local authority so the
costs for the parents are kept down and they are run by a
local management committee in which parents are involved.
Places are in short supply, so you will need to put your
child's name on a waiting list. If you *do* get a place, then you
will find that they offer flexible hours and a high quality of
care. Also, because the local community is involved in their
running, they often pioneer good practice in areas such as
equal opportunities, anti-sexism and anti-racism. In fact,
one advantage of a nursery over a private arrangement with
a childminder or a nanny is that issues of racism and sexism
are much easier to raise as you have a less personal arrangement with the carer.

Private day nurseries have usually been set up as small
businesses and have to run without subsidy. This means that

a place is likely to be expensive as salaries, running costs, other expenses and some profits have to be paid out of the fees that the nursery charges. It is estimated that there are about 30 000 places in private nurseries in the UK, and according to Marion Kozak in her book *Daycare for Kids*, the cost is likely to be around £2500 per annum. Private nursery schools, which provide tuition for children aged 3 and over in school hours, charge about £1500. (Daycare Trust, 1990, pp. 15–16.)

Workplace nurseries have been set up by some employers and, if you are very lucky, you may get a job which will enable you to get a place in one of these. (In 1989 there were about 2000 places in the whole of the UK.) While these may not be a perfect option – you will have to transport a child in the rush hour and you will probably feel tied to staying with the company – they are what many working mothers with young children see as their ideal. How much you will have to pay depends on the subsidy that your employer makes.

How do you decide if a nursery is a good option for your child? The first factor to consider is probably your child's age. While some babies and very young children do settle happily into nurseries, many mothers feel that one-to-one care is more suitable when children are very young. You will need to weigh up both what your child is like and what the nursery is like. Some nurseries do offer very good group care for under-twos; others may not.

Two American researchers, Marilyn Bradbard and Richard Endsley, working together with child experts and mothers, have drawn up a checklist of items that will enable you to judge systematically how good a nursery (or a childminder's home and care) is. The full list is in Alison Clarke-Stewart's book, *Daycare*. Here is a summary of the main items:

HEALTH AND SAFETY

- Adults do not smoke in the same room as the children
- At least one adult is present at all times to supervise children
- Toys and equipment in good repair
- Staff keep records on each child (emergency phone numbers, medical information)

PHYSICAL SPACE

- Dark and quiet space to allow children to nap
- Windows low enough for children to see outside
- Temperature and humidity comfortable
- A variety of visible pictures, posters, mobiles etc
- Toileting area easy for children to get to
- Direct access to enclosed outdoor play area from the building
- Physical space not overcrowded

MATERIALS, EQUIPMENT AND ACTIVITIES

- Materials and equipment for quiet play and active play
- Opportunities to run and climb both indoors and outdoors
- Choice of several activities much of the time
- Toys and play materials available without asking

TEACHERS, ADULT STAFF AND CAREGIVERS

- Adults use encouragement, suggestion and praise rather than orders, commands, prohibitions, criticism or reprimands
- Adults respond to children's questions
- Some sort of educational programme in evidence
- No punishment

CHILDREN

- Children appear happy (laughing, smiling, joking) around adults

- Children are busy and involved and seem to enjoy one another
- No fighting (hitting, pinching, kicking, grabbing toys)
- Children are observed choosing a new activity on their own

PARENTS
- Staff encourage parents to visit and are willing to answer questions and discuss the nursery
- Staff agree with parents about discipline and child management

INDIVIDUAL CHILD
Programme is appropriate for the particular needs and temperament of your child.

PLAYGROUPS

If you are planning to return to work part-time, you may find that you can cover your hours by sending your child to a playgroup. This depends very much on where you live. The majority of playgroups require parents to be involved, so you will need to take your turn on the rota. Hours are very varied too. However, some playgroups are starting to recognise the needs of working mothers and are changing the way they are run to accommodate their needs. You should contact the Pre-School Playgroups Association to see if a group near you might be suitable. (See addresses at the end of this chapter.)

SETTLING YOUR CHILD INTO CHILDCARE

If it is at all possible, you should spend time letting your child get used to the childcare you have found before leaving him or her alone. The best way to do this depends in part on the temperament of your child – on how happy and confident she feels with people she does not know and how quickly she finds her feet in new places. This varies with age too. A child who is unhappy being separated at the age of one may settle very quickly at three. This is how Dawn settled her two-year-old with a new childminder:

> I expected that Sara would not settle easily. We had recently moved house and she was only just getting used to being in a very different place. So I decided to spend as much time as I could settling her in. We visited the new childminder's house together most days over two weeks. Sara was happiest when the childminder's two daughters were home from school. Then, but only then, would she leave my side to go and play. So we agreed that I would leave her for the first time on a Friday when the girls have a half day. Sara did cry when I left for the first few times, but never for long. I decided to leave her for several hours at a time. Once she had settled in the morning, she was happy to stay – I felt it wasn't necessary to leave her for short periods and gradually build up. Now, she is very happy to go, and each morning she chooses some special toys to take and we chat about what she will do and who she will see while I am at work.

Not all young children do settle into the childcare you have found for them and then you will have to weigh up whether you think they will settle in time, or whether you should look for something else. It can be very harrowing to go to work leaving a crying child and to come home to find that the day has gone badly and you had been right to be worried while you were at work. It will have been a harrowing day for the carer too.

I went to pick up my unhappy baby from her childminder

feeling resolved to tell her that I thought the arrangement should end. The childminder agreed and was about to suggest the same thing. You might be able to ask the carer's advice, but you might feel it best to act on your own instincts and change.

On the positive side, if the childcare arrangement is working well, you will feel enormously grateful to your child's carer and she could remain an important person in your child's life well beyond the pre-school years.

CARE FOR SCHOOL-AGE CHILDREN

Many women wait until their children are at school before planning to return to paid work because it is only then that they have time free from childcare responsibilities. Unfortunately, that time very seldom coincides with the hours that employees are expected to work and the headache of finding care for school-age children. As one mother said in the BBC programme *Women Mean Business*:

> There is a myth that you don't have to find childcare
> for children once they start school but actually it's
> much more difficult for most mothers. I find it
> especially hard because I am a single parent and so the
> whole responsibility is on me.

Many women can find no suitable childcare for school-age children. The Kids Club Network estimates that at least one primary school child in six is leaving school to return to an empty home. Tess Woodcraft, speaking on the Channel 4 programme *Who's holding the baby*, reported that:

> We are talking about almost a million children here,
> that's nearly a million parents. They aren't bad parents,

> they are parents who phone two or three times a night,
> they are so worried about what is happening to their
> children. They tell their children not to answer the
> door.

These mothers inevitably worry about their child's welfare and feel guilty and stressed at work. This is how one mother with an 11-year-old daughter copes:

> Obviously when you leave them you have to think
> about things like people coming to the door. I phone her
> about ten times from work until she gets quite annoyed.
> She has been well warned not to open the door to
> anyone. I feel you're torn in two directions, you feel as
> if you're neglecting them really, that you should be
> with them but you've got these commitments . . .
> (SCHOOL'S OUT, SPRING 1990.)

What options do you have? What care is available to cover out-of-school hours and holidays? In practice, it can be quite difficult to find out just what is available in your area. Different schemes will be administered by different departments in your local authority and one department may not know what another department can offer. You should try social services, education, recreation and/or parks services, community affairs, or youth services. You could also try asking at your local school and library. Listed below are the options you might have.

OUT-OF-SCHOOL CLUBS

These offer the best kind of subsidised care that will cover the hours that you are likely to work. Even then, the subsidy is often insecure – less than a quarter have secure funding for the year ahead. There is also a real shortage of places. A survey in 1989 found just over 300 clubs in the UK, providing care for 8500 children during term time and 11 500 over the summer holidays. This means that there are 538 primary school children in the UK for every place in the club. Northern Ireland and Wales are worst served, with more than 600 children per place and Greater London the best, with 133. Denmark, in contrast, has a place for one child in five. (See 'Kid's Clubs Today' in *School's Out*, Spring 1990, pp. 6–7.)

What are after-school clubs? The clubs (or latch-key schemes as they are also known) usually open from 3.30 pm to 6 pm in term time and all day during the holidays. They are held in school buildings, community centres, village halls and purpose-built centres. They are managed and funded in many different ways. Most are run by local community groups or by the local authority. They are staffed by a mixture of paid staff and volunteers, and the average ratio is ten children to each adult in the club. Costs are usually low. In Strathclyde, for example, most people pay less than £10 per week per child. Some schemes give priority to the children of single parents.

What different schemes actually provide does vary, but a good scheme will offer to collect children from school, provide them with a snack and a drink, and keep them happily occupied until the end of the session. This is how the scheme in Darnley in Glasgow is run:

> *The children are escorted both to and from school by a known and trusted adult. While children are in our care we have a legal responsibility for their welfare.*
>
> *As in the home our children are free to do as they wish, be that play – do homework – watch videos – read etc. The project can provide equipment and materials that may not be readily available at home thus widening the children's horizons and*

opportunities. *Parents also benefit as staff provide a non-judgemental ear and support during times of need.*
(Darnley After School Service Information Sheet.)

Parents who use these schemes do seem to be very satisfied with the care they offer. A survey of scheme users in Strathclyde found that 92 per cent were very satisfied and 8 per cent fairly satisfied. They felt that the children were very happy there; their child could mix with other children, and they were always safe and closely supervised. (See Jacqueline Campbell *et al.*, *After School Care – a Survey.* Glasgow College, 1990.)

For many mothers, these schemes mean that they are *able* to be employed or in full-time education. As one mother said in the BBC programme *Women Mean Business*:

Having a playcentre like this isn't just useful for a working mother like me, it's absolutely essential. Because if you look at the number of school holidays that you have, the half terms and everything, there's just no way that you can work full-time, have a child, and not have something like this.

How do you find out if there is a club in your area? In addition to asking your local authority, The Kids Club Network and the Scottish After School Care Association may be able to help. They will also be able to advise you if you decide that the only way to get a club in your area is to start one yourself. Kids Club Network have also published two guides that will help you: *Up, Up and Away* and *Guidelines of Good Practice for Out of School Care Schemes.* (See end of chapter.)

PLAYCENTRES

Playcentres are similar to after-school clubs but offer less supervision and have fewer staff. Usually, children are not registered and are free to come and go as they please. They are usually linked to a local school, and use the school hall and playground. Some authorities run holiday playschemes, using a school, church hall or community building.

ADVENTURE PLAYGROUNDS

Like after-school clubs, adventure playgrounds are also open after school and in the holidays. While adventure playgrounds used to offer little supervision, many have changed in recent years. They usually have an outdoor and an indoor play area and staff on hand to supervise activities. Usually, they do not register children and, as with playcentres, children are free to come and go as they wish. But if you do have an adventure playground near you, it may be worth asking the staff if they would be willing to provide regular care for your child while you are at work. It is worth remembering though that even with supervision, they are really more suitable for older children.

HOLIDAY PLAYSCHEMES

Holiday playschemes only offer care during parts of the school holidays, so they will not solve your problem of out-of-school care. But they could be part of the solution as most working parents find they have to put together a number of different arrangements to cover holiday times. How much of a solution they give varies from area to area. Some just operate for one week in the summer and may close over lunchtime; others are open throughout the summer, Christmas, Easter and half-term holidays.

HOW CAN I TELL IF A SCHEME IS A GOOD ONE?
If you find there *is* a possible scheme in your area then you will need to take a close look to make sure that it offers the kind of care that you and your child will be happy with. You may be able to find out about the scheme from local parents and children who use it and from your child's teacher at school. You will need to phone or write to get basic details and visit with your child so you can judge for yourselves whether it offers an appropriate level of care. The points you will need to look for are:

1   Will the scheme take responsibility for my child, collecting her or him from school and taking her or him there, if a before-school service is offered? Do children remain at the scheme until collected by parents/guardians or a named person?
2   Will the scheme register my child and keep a record of an emergency number, of medical information and details of special needs?
3   Is the scheme safe, both indoors and out? What arrangements have been made for accidents and emergencies?
4   Are there plenty of things for children to do? Is there somewhere quiet for children to go?
5   Do the children and the staff seem happy?
6   Does the scheme cater for the needs of all children from the local community, offering a multicultural approach and taking a positive line on racism and sexism?

INDIVIDUAL SOLUTIONS

Most mothers have to make private arrangements for their children's care out of school hours. Often, they have to make several different arrangements to cover both term-time and holidays. If you also have pre-school children, then you may find that school-age children can be fitted in, with their nanny or childminder picking them up from school.

Most working mothers with school-age children rely on relatives to help them out. Failing that, you will have to employ someone who is not one of the family, perhaps the mother of a school friend, a childminder, a nanny, a mother's help, or an au pair. Whichever of these you choose, you should look back at the sections of this chapter on pre-school care. Much of the advice for and from mothers with young children on employing someone to look after their children will also apply to you.

CHILDMINDERS

Some childminders look after school-age children as well as younger ones. From October 1991 when the new Children's Act comes into force, they will be legally obligated to register with their local social services to look after children under eight years old. You should look back at the earlier section on childminders to see what using a childminder involves, and to explore how to find one to suit your needs.

NANNIES AND MOTHER'S HELPS

A nanny or mother's help is someone who would collect your child from school, give him or her tea and possibly help with your housework until you get back from work. As with childminders, you may need to advertise to find someone, and then interview and follow up references to make sure that you employ someone who you can trust. Again, you should find the earlier section on nannies helpful. Employing a nanny is an arrangement that works well for Isabel:

I have three school-age children and work full-time. I needed to find someone to look after my children out of school hours, in the school holidays, and when they are ill. I advertised for a nanny to work part-time during term-time and full-time during the holidays. We pay her

> £90 per week throughout the year. In term-time, she
> looks after the children between 3 pm and 6 pm and
> does up to 10 hours babysitting. She is also available to
> come in if the children are ill. In the holidays, she looks
> after the children from 8.30 am to 6 pm. While I do
> sometimes resent having to spend so much of my
> earnings on paying someone to look after my children,
> I've found that this is the only arrangement that enables
> me to work full-time with peace of mind. It means that
> the children have continuity of childcare with someone
> they like and trust. We picked someone who they liked,
> and while she isn't very good at washing dishes, she
> does know all about Denis the Menace!

AU PAIRS

If you have room in your house for another person, then you
could consider employing an au pair. An au pair is a young
woman from a European country who comes to live with you
as part of the family. In return for her 'pocket money', she is
expected to help with the children and housework. You
might find yourself with a young women who has a real gift
for working with children and who you completely trust. Or
you may find yourself with a young woman who feels like a
fish out of water, and who needs to be looked after herself.
Either way, you will have certain obligations. Firstly, an au
pair should not work for more than five hours a day.
Secondly, you should tell her in advance what you expect
her duties to be. Thirdly, for your child's sake, make sure
that she speaks and understands English. Fourthly, set the
amount of 'pocket money' she will be given. According to
the *Working Mother's Handbook*, this is usually about £25 a
week or more. Finally, make sure that she has the chance to
attend English classes. If you *do* decide to employ an au pair,
you need to remember that it is only a temporary solution.
Most stay between six months and one year, perhaps filling

in time and improving their English before going to college at home.

If you want to find an au pair, there are specialist agencies who can advise you about terms and conditions. They advertise in the *Lady* and in the Yellow Pages. You could also try a local nanny agency, or enquire at a local language school or college.

In practice, and particularly in holiday time, many working mothers find that they have to make a number of different arrangements for their children. A study of the provision of childcare for children living in London revealed that their mothers made as many as seven different arrangements to get them through the holidays. They adjusted their hours of work, took holidays, took time off without pay, relied on relatives and neighbours, used a playscheme, arranged for their child to go away on a visit and took their child into work. (See Petrie and Logan, *After school and in the holidays: the responsibility for looking after school children.*)

EMERGENCY COVER

There will always be times when your arrangements break down and you need someone or somewhere to fall back on. Your child or your carer may fall ill; your carer may resign or go on holiday; you may have to work unexpected overtime, or the school may unexpectedly close. The *Working Mother's Association* in their *Returners Pack* include the following in their emergency plan:

If your childminder is ill:

- Your carer may have a reciprocal arrangement with a colleague.
- Social services may be able to find you a temporary childminder.
- Join your local babysitting circle and save up tokens. A

mother without a paid job might be able to help you out during the day.

- Get to know other parents of children at your child's school: one of them might be able to help in an emergency.
- Make links with other parents at work: you might be able to help each other out in emergencies.

If your child is ill:

- Invite your mother or mother-in-law for an extended stay.
- Try and change your hours so you can look after your child if she or he is ill.
- Contact a nursing agency for care of a sick child, but be prepared for the cost to be high.

CONCLUSION

The lack of publicly funded childcare in the UK adds considerable stress to the lives of mothers in paid work. Many women stay in their jobs in the hope that combining paid work and motherhood will get easier as children get older. In practice, it seems that the difficulties change and may not lessen until children are well into their teenage years. So if you are thinking of returning to work, it may be a mistake to delay in the hope that once the children are older it will be easier to organise care: now may be as good a time as any. If you *do* go back, you are bound to have mixed feelings about leaving your children in someone else's care. You may feel a sense of loss and be anxious about their welfare. You may feel guilty because you are not at home. But you will probably feel better in yourself for having some time out of the home and some financial independence too. This is how one mother returning to work with a young baby felt:

> *I could use words like happy, confident. And I do feel fulfilled. I've got lots of interesting things to do. I enjoy what I'm doing . . . I was quite excited really by the challenge. It was really quite invigorating to be back and feel I could work again. I felt my old self . . . For my self-esteem it's worked out for the better – to feel I could go back into the same situation and function more or less at the same level even when I'm dog-tired. It's something that's been quite good to do.*
>
> (From *New Mothers at Work*, pp. 122–3.)

You could find that your relationship with your child or children improves too. They may well come to respect you more and feel proud of having a mother who works. You will also be broadening your children's horizons about the kinds of things they might do and expect partners to do when they are grown up. And you may find that your children prefer having someone else look after them some of the time. This is how Laura feels:

> *I quite like having a nanny. She's much younger than mum and good fun. I don't think my mum would like to be in the house all day. She gets bad tempered when she has a lot of housework to do and she's not very good at it.*

FURTHER INFORMATION

USEFUL ADDRESSES

CHILDCARE NOW, THE NATIONAL CHILDCARE CAMPAIGN AND THE
THE DAYCARE TRUST
Wesley House, 4 Wild Court, London WC2B 5AU
Tel: (071) 405 5617/8

CHILDCARE NOW! SCOTLAND
55 Albany Street, Edinburgh EH1 3QY

KIDS CLUB NETWORK
279–281 Whitechapel Road, London E1 1BY
Tel: (071) 247 3009

NATIONAL CHILDMINDING ASSOCIATION
8 Masons Hill, Bromley, Kent BR2 9EY
Tel: (081) 464 6164

PRE-SCHOOL PLAYGROUPS ASSOCIATION
61–63 Kings Cross Road, London WC1X 9LL
Tel: (071) 833 0991

PRE-SCHOOL PLAYGROUPS ASSOCIATION (NORTHERN IRELAND)
Unit 3, Enterprise House, Boucher Crescent, Boucher Road, Belfast BT12 6HU
Tel: (0232) 662825

SCOTTISH CHILD AND FAMILY ALLIANCE
55 Albany Street, Edinburgh EH1 3QY
Tel: (031) 557 2780

THE SCOTTISH PRE-SCHOOL PLAY ASSOCIATION
14 Elliot Place, Glasgow G3 8EP
Tel: (041) 221 4148

THE WORKING MOTHERS' ASSOCIATION
77 Holloway Road, London N7 8JZ
Tel: (071) 700 5771

WORKPLACE NURSERIES CAMPAIGN
77 Holloway Road, London N7 8JZ
Tel: (071) 700 5771

USEFUL BOOKS

- *A Parent's Guide to Childminding*, Sue Owen, National Childminding Association, 1990
- *Babies in Daycare: An Examination of the Issues*, Veronica Williams (ed.), Daycare Trust, 1989
- *Childcare: A Guide to organisations, publications*

research and campaigns concerned with daycare
provision and facilities for young children, Veronica
McGivney, Replan/NIACE, 1990
- *Daycare for Kids: A parents' survival guide*, Marion
  Kozak (ed.), Daycare Trust, 1989
- *Daycare: The Developing Child*, Alison Clarke-Stewart,
  Fontana, 1982
- *The Employer's Guide to Childcare*, The Working
  Mothers' Association
- *Good Working Mothers' Guide*, Mary Beard,
  Duckworth, 1989
- *Guidelines on Childminders' Pay and Conditions from
  April 1990*, National Childminding Association, 1990
- *Guidelines on Good Practice for Out of School Care
  Schemes*, National Out of School Alliance (now Kids
  Club Network)
- *New Mothers at Work*, Julia Brannen & Peter Moss,
  Unwin, 1988
- *School's Out*, Winter 1989/90, Kids Club Network
- *Up, Up and Away: The do-it-yourself guide to setting up
  a kids club and keeping it going*, Kids Club Network,
  1990
- *Women and Employment: A Lifetime Perspective*, J.
  Martin and C. Roberts, HMSO, 1984
- *Working Mothers' Association Returners Pack: A
  practical guide for women returning to work*, The
  Working Mothers' Association, 1990
- *The Working Mother's Handbook: A practical guide to
  the alternatives in childcare*, Working Mothers'
  Association, 1990
- *The Working Mother's Survival Guide*, Jill Black,
  Positive Paperbacks, 1989

CHAPTER SIX

NEW WAYS TO WORK

MARGARET OHREN

Margaret Ohren worked full-time for ten years and spent four years as a student before taking a seven-year career break to bring up her family.

Since then, she has worked part-time and held two job-share posts. She currently works for the organisation New Ways to Work, which promotes flexible working patterns.

INTRODUCTION

The traditional view of home this century has been that of the 'cornflake packet family': mum at home, happy with the children and housework, and dad the breadwinner. Dad was the typical full-time worker: eight-hour days (often longer), forty-eight (or more) weeks a year, a work life of forty or fifty years. Today only 5 per cent of families fit this image, although much of our advertising and the way people think is still based on this myth.

Nowadays 14 per cent of families in Britain are single-parent households and over half of mothers with dependent children go out to work. Not only do women often have to work in order to bring in more income, they increasingly want to work in order to use their skills, education or training.

However, the rigid structure of the full-time working week does not sit easily with the needs of many women with families. It is also a fairly arbitrary arrangement – no one invented the 37- or 40-hour week, it has just evolved!

Many women with dependants – with children or elderly relatives or disabled people to care for – find that they cannot work full-time. Most European countries have concentrated on providing childcare and parental leave schemes to enable mothers to work full-time. In Britain, this is slow to happen.

But while we are behind many of our European partners in providing childcare, other alternatives – such as flexible working arrangements – are being developed here. These arrangements reduce or rearrange the working week so that employees can fit their work around their other responsibilities. As employers try to meet skills shortages by recruiting and retaining more women staff, these options should become more common. In future, women should be in a much stronger position to work the hours that are suitable for them.

This chapter is about ways of making the hours you work more flexible, to suit you. You do not have to work nine to five every day, all year round, and this chapter describes some alternatives. It will give you advice on how to seek these alternatives and on how to ask for them if they are not available. It also looks at the pros and cons of the different arrangements that you can make.

WHAT SORT OF WORK IS AVAILABLE?

PART-TIME WORK

In the past, when many women wished to return to work after having children, they were faced with a choice between full-time and part-time work. While full-time work offered higher pay and possibly chances of promotion, part-time work was at a lower level, and jobs were usually dead end. Often, skilled women had to take very basic jobs such as cleaning or shelf filling in order to get the hours of work they wanted. Although some employers are giving part-timers better conditions these days, much part-time work is still confined to low-paid, low-status, insecure jobs. How many times have you heard a woman describing herself as 'only a part-timer'? She means that her job, and therefore she her-self, is of little account. Why should this smaller number of hours worked make all this difference?

It is not just employers who have given part-time workers lower status – governments have done this too. Many part-time workers have fewer employment rights than people who work full-time. They have divided part-time workers into three categories: people who work less than eight hours a week; people who work less than 16; and people who work 16 or more. People who work 16 or more hours a week have most employment rights. If you work 16 hours or more and you stay with the same employer for two years, you earn the right to redundancy pay, maternity pay, maternity leave and a safeguard against unfair dismissal. Anyone working less than 16 hours a week gets these rights only after five years, and if your hours are less than eight you have no such rights at all. Again, if you work 16 or more hours a week, then after 13 weeks of work you have a right to a written statement itemising your main conditions of employment. But you have to wait five years for this if your hours are below 16. Below eight hours a week you never have this right at all.

Today, the conditions of some part-time jobs are improv-ing, and many are available at 16 or more hours a week. So part-time work may not mean dead-end, low-paid work with no prospects. But you may find that other options which are becoming available offer better conditions and better prospects. Flexible working hours, job-sharing, term-time working, and homeworking or teleworking are becoming increasingly common as employers look to ways to recruit and train women staff. What does each of these entail?

FLEXIBLE WORKING HOURS
OR FLEXITIME

Flexitime is now the most familiar way of providing some flexibility in the working day. Employees are paid to work an allotted number of hours each week or month. There is usually a 'core' time when staff are expected to be at work with the flexible hours fitted on at either end of the day. Any extra hours that people work can be 'banked' for use later on. This can lead to the 'nine-day fortnight' where some local authorities enable staff to work their hours over nine days instead of ten, achieving a regular 'free' day every two weeks.

Employees gain from flexitime by having time to juggle with. Shopping, long lunch-hours, taking children to or collecting them from school can be fitted into a working timetable and additional holidays can be earned by working longer days. But employers gain too, because time taken for visits to doctors and dentists, for instance, comes out of the employee's own time. In addition, punctuality is improved because a few minutes' lateness is added on to the end of the day, or the next day.

Flexitime is popular with employees. A survey of Inland Revenue workers in East Anglia revealed that flexitime was considered to be the biggest single attraction of the job. A national survey of almost 26 000 people carried out in late 1988 found that 35 per cent of the adults questioned said that flexible working hours were likely to be important in their decisions about work in the future.

Clearly, some jobs would not be suitable for flexitime – those with a nine to five responsibility or those jobs which involve working during public opening hours, for instance. However, while flexitime does provide a welcome relief from having to work fixed hours, the total number of hours to be worked is not reduced. Unless flexitime is offered on part-time jobs, it cannot solve the problem of combining employment with looking after children out of school hours.

Cath has a part-time job with flexitime. She works at a doctor's surgery in Bristol. Her job is to set up and maintain a computer system. She works 20 hours each week and she is free to do the work whenever it is convenient to her. It is an arrangement that suits her very well:

> While my children are young, I need to be able to work flexibly. It's worth being paid less in order to have increased flexibility. I can take the children to school in the morning and pick them up again after work. If I want to have time off to go to a school play, or if something urgent crops up, I can rearrange my hours. My only problem is the school holidays when I have to pay for increased childcare.

JOB-SHARING

Job-sharing is a relatively new way of introducing part-time hours into jobs normally reserved for full-time workers. Essentially, it is a very simple concept: two people share one job, dividing the hours and the work between them and sharing the pay, holidays and other benefits. The two people are equivalent to one full-time person. Job-sharers may work mornings and afternoons, two and a half days each, or three short days. They may each be responsible for the whole job or allocate some of the tasks between them. The ways in which the work and time are divided depend on the job itself and on the sharers' preferences.

The range and type of jobs shared is enormous. An A–Z compiled by the organisation New Ways to Work includes many jobs which some people would have thought impossible to share. It includes branch librarians, landscape architects, planners, midwives, social workers, secretaries and teachers; and the number of people job-sharing is growing. Over 2000 people were sharing jobs in local government in 1986, and a survey by the Institute of Manpower Studies in 1989 counted over 500 shared posts in the health service.

Many female job-sharers have found that it is an excellent way to do an interesting job without being tied to full-time hours. This is how Ursula, a College Librarian, described her job-share:

> Certainly, the benefits for me have been enormous: I am no longer frantically trying to juggle two conflicting sets of demands but have time for my son and myself. I also feel I am contributing more to my job. It has been very beneficial to have another professional with whom to share ideas, someone who can cast a fresh eye over existing policies and see ways in which they could possibly be improved. I am equally sure that the college has benefited greatly from having two different personalities with different approaches and with different subject and managerial skills. It has taken a great deal of hard work (and will continue to do so) but the effort has undoubtedly been worthwhile.

Here are the main advantages and disadvantages that job-sharers have found:

ADVANTAGES OF JOB-SHARING

- You can do a high-level job on a part-time basis
- You retain your place on the career ladder
- You should have equal status with full-time workers
- You have a partner to discuss the job with
- You should be able to return to full-time work when you are ready
- You can complement your skills with those of another person

DISADVANTAGES OF JOB-SHARING

- You may find that you tend to work more hours than you are paid for
- You may be treated as 'just a part-timer' and not given full-time status

If you *do* decide that you would like to try a job-share, how would you go about it? Do you need to find your own partner? If you are working full-time and want to job-share, how can you persuade your employer to let you give it a try? If you are looking for a new job, then could you send in a job-share application?

HOW TO GET A JOB-SHARE

APPLYING FOR A JOB-SHARE
It is always worth applying for a job-share, even if a job is advertised as full-time. State in your application that you wish to share the position. Some employers will be willing to rearrange the post or to advertise for a 'second half' in order to gain a valuable recruit.

APPLYING AS A SINGLE JOB-SHARER
Some advertisements for full-time posts state that job-sharers are welcome to apply. You could apply on your own, saying that you wish to share the post. The employer may match you with someone else or even appoint you as a job-sharer and advertise again for the 'other half'.

APPLYING TOGETHER
It is sometimes sensible to apply with someone else and present yourselves as a job-share package; perhaps you or a friend know of someone suitable. For a specialist job, you could try advertising for a partner through a specialist or

professional journal. Alternatively, you could try to find a partner by putting a notice up in your local library or under-fives group, or by writing to members of a local group or trade union.

JOB-SHARE REGISTERS

These are run by some employers, particularly in local authorities. They aim to match you with someone looking for similar work. Ring the personnel department to check. Some professional associations such as those for librarians, housing workers and planners also operate a register for potential job-sharers. New Ways to Work runs a job-share register for people looking for work in the London area.

If you are returning after maternity leave, or wish to reduce your hours, or perhaps if you are just starting with a new employer, you could try to persuade them to let you try job-sharing. Before you start, it would be wise to get all the arguments clear in your mind and to look at some job-share schemes that other organisations have set up. A trade union may be able to help you here. Several unions have published guidelines for members on job-sharing and other flexible options. Among them are Cohse (the Confederation of Health Service Employees), the Health Visitor's Association, and Nalgo (the National and Local Government Officers Association). New Ways to Work also publishes several guides about job-sharing for individuals and for employers. These show good practice and give examples of how job-shares work. New Ways to Work may also be able to put you in touch with someone who is sharing the same job already.

This is how Sheila, who worked as a manager with British Telecom, set about changing her job from a full-time one to a job-share after she returned from maternity leave:

It's a very demanding job and I felt I was not performing in the job as well as I did before. In the end

> *I did full-time for nine months and over that period I
> felt more and more stressed and less and less able to
> cope with the double life. I felt I wasn't doing my job as
> a mother properly and I wasn't doing my job as a
> manager properly and that in itself is stressful. I was
> rapidly coming to the conclusion that the only option
> was to resign and perhaps have a few years away from
> work altogether.*

When her colleague, Ann, became pregnant they researched
job-sharing in other organisations at management level and
prepared a case to show how it would work for them. Then,
fearing rejection, they invited their boss out to lunch.

> *He was very disconcerted by this invitation to lunch . . .
> But he reacted positively straight away 'What a super
> idea, which job are you going to share?'*

In fact, job-sharing does have several advantages for
employers. Here are some arguments that should help
strengthen your case:

ADVANTAGES FOR EMPLOYERS

- You will get two people for the price of one
- Both people come into work fresh
- Two people bring two sets of complementary skills
- You will have greater flexibility, e.g. both people could be
  at work on the busiest day
- You will have continuity of cover, for example when one
  person is off sick or on holiday
- It is simple to arrange
- Most employers with job-sharers are very complimentary

If you *do* find your employer is sympathetic, you might come
to an arrangement and set up an *ad hoc* job-share for your

particular post. However, from everyone's point of view it is best if your employer draws up a job-share scheme for the organisation. This will lay down the rules and offer guidelines to managers on practical issues such as how to divide holidays fairly and how to treat overtime payments, training or car allowances. This will save time in the end and everyone will be treated equally with the same rules applied across the company. Your employer will also be able to add another option to the list of recruitment and retention measures that the company offers.

You should also make sure that you and your job-sharing partner have individual contracts of employment and that the job-share is not dependent on you staying together. If for any reason one partner wishes to leave, then the usual practice is for their half of the post to be offered to the remaining sharer in case they wish to become full-time. If not, then the other half of the post is advertised on a job-share basis.

TERM-TIME WORKING

What to do about the holidays is a major headache for women with school-age children. While flexitime and job-sharing can ease the stress and difficulties of combining family responsibilities and paid employment, working hours are still very unlikely to match the hours that children are in school. School holidays are a headache because they last longer than most people's annual leave and are even longer than two parents' holidays added together. School holidays add up to about 14 weeks a year but average leave entitlement is between four and six weeks plus bank holidays. This means that there are about seven or eight weeks a year when parents need to be at work and children are not at school. A term-time-only working arrangement is one solution. As companies experience labour shortage, more of these schemes are being set up. How do these schemes work?

The Dixon's Stores Group introduced their scheme in November 1988 to encourage more women returners and also to change the age profile of store staff. Employees working term-time only have a contract for 41 weeks. They have the same conditions of work as full-timers, and are paid the *pro rata* rate. Like full-timers, they are entitled to sick pay, and they attend the same training and induction courses as full-time colleagues. They must take their holidays during school holidays, but in addition there is provision for two weeks' unpaid leave at other times to allow for the care of sick children at home.

The Alliance and Leicester Building Society also has a term-time working scheme, aimed at parents of children between 5 and 14 years of age. Women can take ten weeks' unpaid leave a year and are expected to take four weeks of their holiday entitlement during school holidays. Salary is paid continuously during the year and term-time workers are entitled to the full range of staff benefits such as sick pay, pension and the concessionary mortgage scheme.

Boots the Chemist also offers term-time-only working as part of a package to recruit and retain female staff. This includes flexible working and part-time hours. This woman was drawn to Boots by their policy of offering term-time-only working:

> *I moved new into the area and I was looking for work which fitted around my children. A friend told me that Boots were advertising for term-time-only people – this means that when half-term arrives I can be away from work.*

It was part-time hours, combined with term-time working, that attracted this woman:

> *I work within the hours of 9.45–2.30 which means that*

I can take my children to school and pick them up again – it's great. It means that I can combine my work and home responsibilities, and I have all the benefits of full-time staff.

HOMEWORKING OR TELEWORKING

Perhaps instead of travelling to work each day you would really prefer to be paid to work at home. Homeworking is still associated with the long hours and low pay of machinists, Christmas cracker makers and envelope writers. But the possibilities of working at home have been greatly increased by the introduction of new technology and telecommunications, which make it possible to link people at home with their workplace, fairly cheaply. Teleworking, telecommuting, remote or homeworking are arrangements where salaried employees spend all or some of their working week at home or working from home.

Today, the range of jobs that people do around a home base is really quite broad, and up to 2 million people are estimated to work in this way. Engineers, roving sales staff and equipment repairers are examples of people who work from home, using it as a base to go out to work. Journalists, writers, researchers, accountants, clerks and other administrative staff are all people who are increasingly working at home. By the mid-1990s, it has been predicted that as many as 4 million people could be 'teleworking'.

Among the larger companies which operate teleworking are International Computers Ltd (ICL), ICI Agrochemicals, Shell, BP and the FI Group. ICL and the FI Group employ computer staff from home. Both companies use a pool of professional women with family commitments who also wish to continue their careers as trained computer experts. They often work on projects for client organisations based

miles away or even on the other side of the country. The FI Group is now aiming to open a system of work centres as back-up for their home-based staff.

Gill is an example of a homeworker who is employed by ICL. She is a technical author, writing computer manuals and guides for people who use computers. She is paid to work for 25 hours per week and she can do these hours whenever she wants to. In practice, she has developed a routine, and she tends to work the same hours each week. Gill describes the way that she organises her work at home.

> It's very free and flexible. I do need to be very
> disciplined and it did take a while to get into a routine.
> But I like being in charge of myself. If I want to do my
> work on a Sunday, or if my children are unwell, or I
> want to go and see a school play, I just rearrange my
> hours. Some people find this way of working lonely,
> but I don't. You get used to not going anywhere.

Local councils and smaller non-computer companies are introducing teleworking too. The London Borough of Enfield, for example, has taken on homeworkers to deal with the clerical demands of the community charge. They employ 72 staff who work from their homes on computer terminals provided by the council. They are mainly engaged on data entry work: extracting information from forms and entering it into the council's computer system. They are paid the same money *pro rata* as other employees based at the council's offices doing the same job.

While working at or from home may sound attractive, it is important to weigh up the pros and cons first.

ADVANTAGES

- You avoid the morning and evening rush hours
- You save the costs and time of travelling
- You are closer to your children
- You can fit your paid work around your domestic work more easily, hanging out the washing or slipping out for the shopping when you need a break

DISADVANTAGES

- You will need to discipline yourself to get the work done
- You may find it hard to judge how much you need to do in a day and overcompensate by working too much
- You may miss the social contact that going out to work provides
- You may feel isolated
- You may wish that you were more closely supervised
- You will have higher bills due to the fact that you are at home rather than at work
- You will need to have a space where you can work undisturbed

In practice, many companies will not leave you completely

on your own. They will keep in touch by telephone and hold regular meetings, and possibly social functions too. None the less, you will be on your own for much of your working time.

FINDING FLEXIBLE WORKING OPPORTUNITIES

As employers change their working practices, it can be hard to know who offers flexible working and who does not. A recent IPM survey found that 37 per cent of companies were taking steps to encourage women back to work. (See *Work and the Family. Carer-Friendly Employment Practices,* Dorothy Berry Lound.) Their measures included introducing part-time or flexible hours, making creche or childcare provisions, offering career breaks, job-sharing, career resumption training, extended maternity leave or term-time contracts. So it could be that a job you are interested in is open for flexible working of some kind.

Look at job advertisements, sometimes a part-time, flexitime or job-share post is advertised.

It is also worth looking at the small print in advertisements. Many employers, particularly in the public sector, advertise themselves as 'equal opportunity' employers and this may mean that they either have a policy about, or they will employ people wishing to work, flexible hours. Ring or write to the personnel department, or the manager in charge, to ask. Many charities or voluntary organisations are more than willing to offer flexible hours since they often cannot compete in other ways with private employers.

It is always worth applying for a job which you would like to do, but which is only advertised as full-time – write an application and say, perhaps in a covering letter, what hours or time you can offer.

In addition, there are now a few professional recruitment

or employment agencies which specialise in placing people looking for part-time work or work offering flexible hours. A list of some of these is available from New Ways to Work. In addition, the larger high street recruitment agencies are increasingly persuading employers to create flexible opportunities and offer training courses and help with applying for posts, attending interviews etc. Call in and ask.

Above all try not to be afraid to ask for what you want. You are in demand at the moment. There is a national skills shortage and a fall in the number of young people available for training. Sensible employers are very much aware of this and are willing to listen and rearrange the traditional structures and working arrangements in order to make use of the time you are able to give.

There are some final points for you to weigh up before deciding the kind of arrangement that would suit you best.

- Is it worthwhile financially to work less than full-time?
- How much do I need to earn to compensate for any benefits I may lose? Remember to take into account non-cash benefits such as free prescriptions and free passes.
- How much extra money will I need to cover the costs of working – travel, clothes, lunches?
- As a part-timer or job-sharer, would I be eligible for the company pension scheme?

CONCLUSION

As more of the workforce, and particularly more women, start to work the hours which suit them, the stereotyped image of the nine to five worker will start to crumble – around the edges at least. The worlds of work and home, which previously never met, may come closer together. This could lead to other changes in work practices too. Many working women have to cope with very tight timetables. They often have not got the option of staying at meetings which are running late, and cannot take on unscheduled extra work after hours. In fact part-time or job-sharing staff can often highlight inadequacies and inefficiencies in the full-time system. In many jobs, because of the constraints of their hours, they turn out to be more productive and efficient than their colleagues!

Thus it may be that the workplace will have to change so that schedules are planned more efficiently, out-of-hours meetings are abandoned, and communications systems are better organised and come to rely less on word of mouth. In the end, most people would benefit if we were judged on how well we work in the hours we are paid for, and not on how many hours we put in.

FURTHER INFORMATION

USEFUL ADDRESSES

HACKNEY JOB SHARE
Shoreditch Town Hall, 380 Old Street, London EC1V 9LT
Tel: (071) 739 0741
NEW WAYS TO WORK
309 Upper Street, London, N1 2TY
Tel: (071) 226 4026
MANCHESTER AREA JOB SHARERS
c/o 11 Sidbury Road, Chorlton, Manchester M21 2XN
Please write, marking your correspondence 'Manchester Area Job Sharers'.

USEFUL BOOKS

- *Hours to Suit*, Anna Alston and Ruth Miller, Rosters, 1989, £4.95
- *Job Sharing: An Introductory Guide*, New Ways to Work, £1.50
- *Job Sharing: A Practical Guide*, Pam Walton, Kogan Page, £6.99 from bookshops or £7.99 from New Ways to Work
- *Job Sharing Employment Rights and Conditions*, New Ways to Work, £1.50
- *Job Sharing: Nalgo negotiating guidelines*, Nalgo. From Nalgo, 1 Mableton Place, London WC1H 9AJ, free, but 20p postage
- *Job Sharing: Putting policy into practice*, New Ways to Work, £6.00
- *Work and the Family: Carer Friendly work practices*, IPM, 1990

SEVEN

WORKING FOR
YOURSELF

CHRISTINA HARTSHORN

Christina Hartshorn is the Enterpriser Officer for Women in Scotland. Born in Birmingham in 1946, she first trained and practised as a Careers Adviser. She has lived in Holland, Greece and Abu Dhabi, where she started to bring up her family.

Now based at the University of Stirling, she was awarded an Equal Opportunity Fellowship by the German Marshall Foundation in 1987 when she travelled extensively in the United States reviewing business provision for women.

INTRODUCTION

I gave up my original career in computing to bring up my family. Out of a long-held interest I started to study herbalism but because of family commitments did not manage to finish the course of study. My children were by now in their teens, my husband's job often took him away and elderly relatives needed support. I did not want to return to computing and felt that no one would employ me because I had no other skills.

I wondered if I could start a business selling dried medicinal herbs. In the age of the tea-bag would I find people prepared to make their own medicines? I felt I would need to lay out a large amount of money for stock and no one would lend me money without a business plan. Feeling discouraged I wondered how I could learn to be 'capable' of running a business for myself.

Various groups in the area had asked me to give talks on herbalism and I found that there was a demand for a beginners' book, so I started to write one and desktop published it myself. Then I realised that here was a skill

I could turn into a business, but what did I know about running a business? Nothing.

I noticed an advertisement in the local paper for a business course for women which included writing a business plan. My confidence level was still low and I did not think I would get on the course, but I did and found for the first time in years that I could focus attention on me! As the course progressed I began to realise just how many skills I did have.

Other course members were ready customers and I was very fortunate when two of the course lecturers gave me my first large job, desktop publishing their training manual. Other work steadily followed and, alerted by a friend, I made a successful bid for a substantial contract with a large organisation. When I am busy I subcontract some of the work. I choose to work from home so I can continue to fulfil my family commitments. Enlarging the business is important. I'm ploughing back as much as I can in order to buy better equipment and hope to take on my first employee soon.

Working for yourself means you can run things your own way. As for thinking I had no skills, well just by being responsible for so many things over all those years I had developed basic skills in budgeting, stock control, forward planning and decision-making – abilities which most women in the home have developed without realising it and exactly the skills I needed to tackle desktop publishing problems creatively and meet business deadlines.

Rhona, Unicorn Publishing

Rhona, like many thousands of women, returned to work last year having previously been at home bringing up her family. Unlike the majority of those women who went back to work, however, Rhona created her own job. In fact although working for yourself is still a minority activity, it is the fastest-growing sector of the economy, and all over the country women are turning to self-employment as never before. We see women working on their own or with others, in partnerships, co-operatives, limited companies and community businesses. Whatever form their business takes, they have one factor in common, they are all creating their own employment.

Working for yourself is not an easy option. In fact, going into business can be very complex, with many factors to consider and a welter of detail to pick through – markets, equipment, staff, premises and the dreaded finance and book-keeping – to name but a few. There is too much to cover in the space here, but this chapter will help you to take those important first steps. We are going to look at the reasons for going into business, why *you* in particular might want to, how the skills and talents you have can be used in a business and how you take the next crucial steps beyond your initial thoughts.

At the end of the chapter there is a list of books and organisations which will help with the practicalities, and suggestions about where you might get support and encouragement.

WHY GO INTO BUSINESS?

As we have said before, working for yourself is still relatively uncommon for women – of every 13 women who work, only one works for herself whereas one in six working men work on their own account. People often find it unusual to see a woman running a business and sometimes make unhelpful or patronising comments about her. This is why it is important for you to have a clear understanding of your reasons for wanting to work for yourself. Whatever your reason, stick to it and don't be put off by negative comments. At the outset there is no 'right' reason for wanting to start up in business. There are as many reasons as there are women in business – what matters is that it is right for you.

Rhona had a mixture of reasons for wanting to start up in business, some positive, some negative. She wanted to do something for herself that had nothing to do with the family, but would not stop her from being a wife and mother. However, she was fearful that no employer would want her after her years at home. She felt she had no skills to offer an employer.

But there are lots of other reasons why women have wanted to work for themselves.

I want to turn an idea into a business
I want to control the hours I work and when I work them
I want to be able to work and look after my family
I want to provide jobs for my family
I want to work with other women
I want to work for something that really matters to me
I want to provide jobs for other people
I want to be the boss
I want to make money
I'm bored
I'm too old to do anything else – no one wants to employ me
I can't find any work around here
You can't get these products here
No one offers this service here
People are paying me for things I make as a hobby

Do you recognise any of these reasons? Having a clear idea of your motives for wanting to work for yourself will keep you going when the going becomes tricky.

HAVE I GOT WHAT IT TAKES TO RUN A BUSINESS?

Knowing your reasons for wanting to go into business *will* keep up your determination to succeed; however, being motivated is not enough on its own. You need particular skills and talents. Before you can answer the question 'have I got what it takes?' you have to know what running a business involves and what skills and talents you *do* have to bring to a business.

Businesses have many assets or resources – for example premises, materials, staff, a full order book. The greatest resource a small business has, however, is its owner – you. It is therefore essential to spend time looking at the 'you' resource in some detail, to see how your skills and talents relate to running a business. Many women freeze at this point, thinking that they do not have any, especially if they have been at home for several years, and as Rhona discovered, long absence from paid work really saps your confidence.

Take this chance to look positively at all the things you *have* done rather than concentrating on the gaps. What you are trying to do is consider, first of all, your ability to run a business and only secondly to run a *specific* business. There are key elements which are common to all businesses, from chemical processing to running a creche.

Here is an exercise to complete to help you unpackage the abilities you have as an aspiring business owner. This was Rhona's first lesson on her business start-up course.

LOOK AT ME!

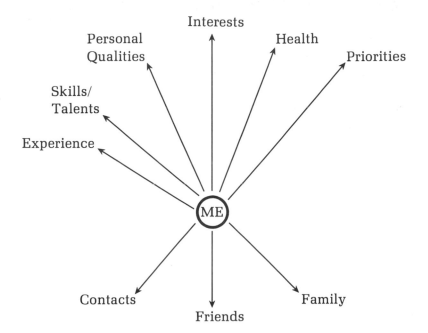

Starting with Experience, look at each item in turn. Take a piece of paper and start to write about yourself.

Look closely at the experiences you have had outside paid work. Perhaps you have been the organiser of the baby-sitting group or treasurer of the playgroup. Look especially at areas where you have organised people and things, managed money and time, and generally made things happen. These are the everyday skills you need to run a business. A Jill-of-all-Trades, working for yourself means being able to do everything yourself and often all at the same time. Does this sound familiar?

Look at how life has qualified you to do many things. Don't limit yourself to bits of paper gained at school.

Complete the sentence 'I know how to . . .' or 'I can . . .' Do it at least ten times. You end up with a list which might contain items like this:

'*I can plan, organise and manage a three-week foreign holiday for five people, age range 4 to 42.*' This is the annual family camping holiday to mainland Europe which involves route planning, liaising with suppliers (travel agents), task management, financial budgeting, contingency planning and so on.

'*I know how to listen.*' Encouraging friends to talk about their *real* needs. Business owners must be able to hear what their customers *really* need and so provide products and services that meet them.

'*I know how to start up and run a playgroup.*' Persuading others to join you, providing leadership for the group, acquiring premises and resources, ensuring high standards of safety and quality of play equipment, innovating new features, motivating others. All of these skills and experiences are needed in running a business.

Dounne used her experiences of life in the management of her business, Gramma's Herbal Pepper Sauce,

I decided to take the risk during the lowest period of my life, where my marriage had just broken down. I moved into a council flat, I had to redecorate a suitable home for my daughters. Then through financial problems, not having enough money to survive, my eldest daughter suggested, 'why not market the sauces that you make?' I managed because I think women as a whole are the best organisers. We have been trained from birth to manage, take responsibility of a home, to take care of others, and so in my entire job I have simply used this same method of being the best manager of my own home. I motivated my own self, my children, I find it very, very easy, because my children are totally

supportive and co-operative. If I can't motivate them,
then I can't motivate anyone else.

Now look at your personal qualities. By this we mean attributes such as determination, perseverance and optimism. How flexible is your thinking and how do you judge situations? How would you describe your personality – hot-tempered, outgoing, thoughtful, loyal? Write down the words that describe you.

Running a business calls for a determined nature. It is worth remembering that from the outset and perhaps for some while, there will be just you to do everything. Look for examples of your qualities from your everyday life. Can you stick to a task? Can you put everything else aside and work towards achieving something important? Are you someone who does not take no for an answer or who keeps asking questions until you are sure you understand an instruction or concept? When your child was in pain did you seek out a second and third opinion until the cause of her pain was discovered and treated? Of course you did. This is the sort of perseverance, determination and desire to solve problems that you will need for your new business.

In business some women find it hard at first to collect outstanding payments owed to them for goods and services they have provided. Somehow it does not seem to be quite acceptable to pursue others for money owed, but unless you act assertively, your business will fail through lack of cash. You have done the work, the money is yours.

It is also important to reflect on what really interests you. There is no merit in setting up a business, even though you may be good at it, if it is based on something you are not interested in doing. You have to be enthusiastic about your business because you will need to enthuse others to gain their ongoing support. Examining your interests may also generate business ideas. Rhona's interests gave her two business ideas, selling dried medicinal herbs and desktop publishing.

Now look at your state of health and say honestly whether you have any health problems. In a one-person business, if you are off sick the consequences for the business can be catastrophic. Even a short illness can cause a setback. Even if you have no health problems it is worth considering the stresses and strains that running a business generates and ensuring that you have the means in other areas of your life to reduce the stress and relax. This is an important point which is often overlooked. Running your own business can start to dominate your life very easily – you need to be prepared for this.

The item on priorities relates to how much of the business you want in your life and how much of your life you want in your business. How important is running a business to you? What in your life might you have to give up or put on hold whilst you devote your energies and commit resources to your growing business?

All of the items so far relate to the internal you, and your personal abilities, skills, experiences and priorities that you can bring to a business. The next three items focus on your immediate world and how it can help you move forward as a business owner.

Firstly, look at your family. Women have found their families to be tremendously supportive, giving not only moral support and encouragement but practical help within the business and also at home. Family members have helped to redecorate and refurbish business premises, and they are another pair of hands when the business is up and running. One antique dealer arranged her stock buying for the two mornings a week her mother offered to run the shop. Childcare is also often supplied by willing grandparents.

You may have young children, you may also have dependent older members of the family. What will be the impact of the business on them and then in turn on you? Many women experience conflict at this point – conflicts of time, expectations and responsibilities – all of which can lead to a sense of guilt and frustration.

This is the time to discuss things honestly and clearly with your family. Without their *positive* support, working for yourself will not be impossible, but it will be more difficult. Set out your reasons for wanting to work for yourself, what you want out of the business and how you see the business operating. The negotiating techniques you use at this point to draw up family operating guidelines will be good practice for running your business!

Secondly, you should consider your friends. Women often call upon their friends as much as their families for moral and practical support. Friends may also help with childcare or provide the business with skills that you do not possess. However, friendships may well be stretched as you find you do not have the time to maintain them. As only a minority of people work for themselves, the chances are that friends will not comprehend the amount of time you will be having to devote to the business.

Finally, women often have contacts without realising it, for example, with the mother and toddler group, the local church or sports club. Think about which groups you belong to and think of how you can use them to help your business grow. Try not to shy away from the word 'use', it is not meant in a grasping, selfish way. We spoke earlier about how your enthusiasm for your business is infectious. Talk to your 'contacts' about your business and there is a chance that someone will know someone who might be a potential customer, or supplier. You might also test out your business idea on people you know to see if there is a market for it. Or their needs may spark off new ideas and get you moving in a different direction – it was from her herbalism contacts that Rhona first embarked on desktop publishing.

Look back at what you have written about yourself and your immediate world. Think of who and what will help your business go forward. Can you see anything that might hold it, or you, and therefore the business, back? Work out plans to strengthen your plus points and overcome your minus points.

Looking more particularly now at your ability to run a *specific* business, you need to go back to the item on skills and talents. Check out what practical or technical skills you have, and how good these skills are. For example, Rhona had high-level computer skills which she was able to use as the technical base of her business. She still needed extra training with certain software packages, but she was able to form her business around an existing skill. Once again, do not limit yourself only to jobs and tasks that you have been paid to do in the past. You may have an amazing talent for organising events or persuading people to do things, as shown by producing a Gang Show or staging a village fête. Complete as many 'I can . . .' statements as you can. You will be amazed at how long the list is. Running a business is often about seeing old things in new ways. Your trick must be to transform old and therefore probably undervalued skills into business opportunities.

MY BUSINESS IDEA

Having thought through your reasons for wanting to run a business and established that you do have what it takes to run one, the next step is to check out your business idea. Have you got an idea? Do not give up if you have not got one. Most businesses do not start with a new invention, they are usually a tried and tested idea, or a variation on an existing idea. This list might give you some ideas.

- A business based on a product or service that people want but is not being offered in your area.
- A business based on a product or service that *you* want but no one anywhere is making or selling.
- A business based on the products of your hobby or craft that people are now wanting to buy.
- A business based on skills or experience you have from previous paid or unpaid work.
- A business based on resources you already possess and can use in new ways e.g. a spare room, a camera, a car.

Pat started her business, Solutions, from previous career experiences.

My training in social work and my experience of developing a personnel counselling service for 14 000 employees in a large organisation gave me a good idea for a business. I now provide consultancy and training services for employees intending to set up their own counselling schemes and also provide an independent employee counselling service for companies which are too small to have their own.

Jane expanded Kinnaird Pottery using existing resources.

Pottery was my hobby and became my business. I turned an old outbuilding into a pottery and saleroom. Later on I started to use a large loft area as a dormitory for students so that I could expand into Learn to Pot summer courses.

Do not be put off if you have not got a specific idea, you just have to put in some work to generate a few. Look at *everything* you do for a week with an eye for a business idea.

Fiona based her business, An Occasional Stitch, on a craft hobby.

> I'd been brought up in a home where handcrafts were a
> way of life. I trained as a Registered General Nurse and
> midwife and worked to gain experience. I put my
> career on hold to have my children but then found it
> inconvenient to return. Spending more time in
> handcrafts over the past few years I found friends were
> regularly ordering counted cross-stitch samplers and
> records to commemorate family celebrations. It is very
> satisfying to create something that gives others such
> pleasure. I wondered if I could possibly turn this hobby
> into a way of working for myself. I could and I did.

Attune your mind to looking at every situation you are in,
from an ideas point of view. Have ideas sessions with
friends where everyone chips in. Concentrate on collecting
as many ideas as possible. Do not stop to think whether it is a
good idea or not, you can do that later.

Moira set up Ullapool Tapestry Enterprise after an initial
personal setback.

> The community wanted to celebrate its two hundredth
> anniversary with something tangible. We decided to
> stitch a tapestry with 200 scenes depicting life in the
> area over the past two centuries. The idea grew that we
> could sell postcards and posters of the tapestry and use
> the profits to benefit the folk of Ullapool.
>
> I had been on a business start-up programme and
> learned how to write a business plan, but the particular
> business idea I had, foundered. When I got back to
> Ullapool I realised that I could put all this business
> knowledge to use in the community. Four of us are now
> working together as Ullapool Tapestry Enterprise, a
> Community Business, each contributing our own
> special skills and talents. The Enterprise fosters self-
> help and binds the community together – something

we've always done up here anyway. We're making and marketing a range of products based on the Tapestry and all the profits are going towards financing a community swimming pool. I've now written that business plan and used it to raise money from the Local Employment Initiatives fund to buy equipment for the business.

Your first idea for a business is often transformed into something quite different by the time your business takes off. Rhona's ultimate desktop publishing business bore no resemblance to her original idea of selling dried medicinal herbs. There is a fine line between being single-minded about an idea in order to take it forward and being so protective of it that you do not allow it to grow and develop.

GETTING HELP

Now you have decided what sort of business you are interested in, what is the next step? All the steps that have been described above are ones that you can do on your own or with family and friends. You can do the rest on your own too, if you want to, but you might find it easier to plug into the help network that exists for aspiring business owners. It was at this point, in fact, that Rhona looked about for some help. What did she know about business? In common with most would-be owners, nothing. Some women find this moment difficult. 'It's just a hobby . . .', 'I only want to work from home . . .', 'I don't know anything about business . . .' are often opening remarks women make when they talk to someone from the business world for the first time about their idea.

Many women have been made to feel that since they were starting a business in a very small way or on a part-time basis, then that activity somehow did not count as a business. Remember that it is your choice to do it this way, you are in control of it and it is just as much a real business as job-sharing or part-time work is real work. Also, there is much to be said for starting small and building up the business slowly at a pace that fits in with other aspects of your life. You do not have to make the great leap from being at home full-time to challenging Anita Roddick in one bound. For example, many women returners nurse the idea of working for themselves whilst gaining experience of the working world as an employee.

There has never been more help on offer to start a business than there is today. There are so many organisations offering different kinds of help. In fact there is so much information containing so many new terms, that it can be very confusing to the newcomer – the very person to whom all this help is so carefully aimed!

To simplify things, there are four broad types of assistance to be found in the business help network: advice and support, training, information and finance.

ADVICE AND SUPPORT

Running a business can be quite lonely if the business consists of just you. Finding a business adviser or counsellor before you start up is a good way to overcome that particular difficulty. Individual business counselling is free and available from many sources. One-to-one sessions are especially helpful as you can set the agenda and pace. You are often able to build up a relationship with your adviser who can give you moral support and encouragement when you need it as well as particular advice on specific topics, such as marketing, pricing, locating premises. Business advisers or counsellors work from Enterprise Agencies and Trusts, local authority Economic Development Units, the Small Firms Service and specialist Women's Enterprise organisations. See the end of the chapter for useful addresses.

Enterprise Agencies and Enterprise Trusts are local organisations which have been set up to help small businesses start up and grow. There are over 300 of them all over the country and they are staffed by a small core of permanent employees and a larger number of specialist business advisers who work on a part-time or consultancy basis. They are an invaluable source of support, information and advice, and you should visit them sooner rather than later. Their services are, in the main, free.

Often in the early stages of thinking about a business women are reluctant to see a male business counsellor. They think their idea will be dismissed as silly or not a real business. Most business counsellors are men, but with more and more women coming forward to start businesses male advisers are becoming more familiar with the kind of problems women face and are therefore able to give the right kind of advice. If you think your adviser has not taken you seriously, ask to see another one to check out your thoughts and ideas. Unfortunately there are still very few women working as business advisers. If you are having difficulty finding a business adviser in your area, because names and titles may change, try your local Citizens' Advice Bureau or the local library. They should be able to refer you to the right person or advisory group.

Once in business, owners often join self-help groups for support. Traditional business networks – for example Chambers of Commerce and Rotary – are, in the main, run by men with men in mind. Women business owners have sometimes found it difficult to utilise the advantages that stem from membership of these organisations. Some women have overcome this hurdle by starting business networks of their own, for mutual support and encouragement. There are names and addresses of some of these groups at the end of the chapter.

TRAINING

Research has shown that people who have undergone some form of training for running their own business and used business advisers at the outset stand a better chance of success. Everything that has been said in this book about preparing to return to work also applies to those of you who want to work for yourselves. Even aspiring business-owners can be filled with self-doubt about their ability to start up and run a business. General courses and exercises in confidence-building such as those suggested in chapter 1 can be a very valuable starting point for women who want to work for themselves. It is worth repeating that *you* are the greatest resource your business possesses, so do all you can to understand and develop this resource before you start the business.

Training courses for business start-up are to be found throughout the country. On a training course you can expect to spend time assessing yourself, your skills and your business idea as well as learning new business skills and acquiring knowledge in business topics such as marketing, finance and business planning. Tutors will assume you know nothing and work at a pace to suit you. If they do not, then *tell* them and ask them to set you examples you can work through at home until you do understand.

Some organisations provide women-only courses of training which give those women who have been away from the workplace for some time, the chance to develop themselves and their business idea in a women-friendly atmosphere. The course that Rhona joined, Enterprise Training for Women at Stirling University, was designed to meet the needs of women returners. It lasts for ten weeks. Three days a week (hours to fit school timetables) are in class, learning about market research, business planning, finance, marketing and so on. The other two days are spent away from class and are taken up with planning the individual business, meeting suppliers, finding customers and writing the business plan. Tutors on the programme are a mix of university staff, local women business-owners, bank officials and other outside specialists. By the end of the programme, participants will have written their own business plan.

Training programmes help your confidence to grow in two

ready know from
nent with Parent
y teach you new
g is usually free
e Agencies and
especially set up
ed through ET in
prise Agency or

s starts, there are
pecific business
eting, customer
nanagement, are

APPOINTMENT CARD
LAURIE PIKE HEALTH CENTRE
95 BIRCHFIELD ROAD

YOUR NEXT APPOINTMENT IS

AY	DATE	TIME	TO SEE
IURS ·	22/03 ·	15·00	NURSE

IF YOU ARE UNABLE TO KEEP YOUR APPOINTMENT PLEASE TELEPHONE HE SURGERY ON **523 8111/554 0621**

INFORMATION

Most high street banks and large firms of chartered accountants produce booklets and information packs aimed at new business-owners. These packs provide you with a rich source of new vocabulary, terms, checklists and business forms. Becoming familiar with business terms is an important way of increasing your confidence. After you have had

initial discussions with a business adviser about whether
working for yourself is right for you, it is worth reading
through a selection of these booklets to reflect on your next
steps. Most branches of banks and accountants will be able
to supply you with booklets, but it is especially useful to
check out those who label themselves as business branches.
Your local library should also have a good selection of books
on how to start up in business. (See the list at the end of this
chapter for details.) Accountants and bankers themselves
give business information and advice, but they can often be
used to better effect once you have a clearer picture of what
you want from working for yourself. Most Enterprise
Agencies and Trusts give general business information as
well as advice and counselling. They will also provide information about training for business start-up and for business
growth, and for any schemes which help you over specific
problems such as marketing. Some run Small Business
Clubs, providing a room where new business-owners can
meet each other informally and exchange ideas, news, help
and support. Larger agencies might also manage small business units – premises at low-cost rents for up to a year to help
more businesses to start up. They might also have a busi-
ness-to-business service, a computerised matching facility
to put local suppliers and buyers in touch with each other.

Your local council may also have an economic development unit which will give you information on business premises, local by-laws relating to business and any special
schemes they may run to encourage new businesses. The
Government's Small Firms Service has a free telephone
helpline to put you in touch with people who can give information and advice.

FINANCE

Banks and accountants are the two organisations that would-be business-owners frequently turn to for help about money. Once again, you will probably get more out of an interview with them if you have done some homework first such as reading their booklets. Business advisers from the Enterprise Agencies and Trusts will also be able to tell you about other ways of raising finance, if that is what you need. There are many kinds of loans and grants available now although whether you can apply for them depends on many factors, for example your age, location, type of business and whether you employ others. It is vital that you check out your eligibility for a loan or grant with a business adviser *before* you start trading, otherwise you might find that you have missed a chance of extra funding for your business.

❷❷❸

WRITING A BUSINESS PLAN

Rhona knew it was important to have a business plan even though initially she did not know exactly what it was. A business plan is a statement about what you intend to do, how you are going to do it and what resources you need to do it. It is important to capture your thoughts and work on paper because if you do not then your thoughts of working for yourself will remain just that – thoughts.

Writing a business plan is a discipline. It makes you take a step back from your idea and look at it objectively. A business plan has three purposes.

- It forces you to set down your ideas on paper.
- It gives you the basis against which you can monitor the progress of your business.
- It can help you raise finance for the business.

You should write the business plan yourself. Ask for information and advice from your business advisers but do not let anyone else write it. *You* are the one who has found the information, done the leg work, and the plan is *yours*. Writing the plan gives you confidence in your business as nothing else can.

WHAT IS IN THE BUSINESS PLAN?

The business plan should describe:

- What your business does.
- Your product or service and how you are going to produce or provide it.
- The market for your products or services. Who are you selling to? Competitors and your advantages over them.

- The management team. Your experience and abilities to *manage* the business.
- Resources needed. For example, equipment, premises and key staff. Their abilities to make and sell the products or services (it could be you again).
- The financial state of the business. The current position. How much money does the business need, for what purpose? Where will this money come from. What if . . . ?

You can write the business plan on plain paper, but many people find the printed business plan booklets, which are available from business support agencies or the banks, very helpful. In supplying answers to their pre-printed questions, you find that you have ended up with a completed business plan. Let us now look a little more closely at each of those areas that must be included in the business plan.

WHAT YOUR BUSINESS DOES
All business is about making a profit from satisfied customers. Try to summarise yours in a sentence like this 'Sally's Sandwiches will provide and deliver, at a profit, quality lunches to office workers within a one-mile radius of Bristol Main Post Office'.

PRODUCING AND DELIVERING YOUR PRODUCT
How are you going to make and deliver your product? Are you going to make everything yourself or buy in some components or skills? Do you comply with trade standards? How will you ensure consistency and quality? Will your customers be the people who use the product or will you sell to a middle-person, such as a wholesaler? How will your customers know about your product? All of these areas need careful thought and research – it is a key part of your business.

CUSTOMERS

However inventive, attractive or desirable your product, you have to provide something that people want to buy at a price that gives you a living. You must test out your idea on potential customers to make sure you have a market. This is usually known as doing the market research. It means finding out what the market is for your product. Who are the customers? Where are they? How many of them are there?

You do not need to stand on rainy street corners with a clipboard asking people directly whether they will buy your product. There are many other ways of getting information without getting wet. See the booklist at the end of the chapter for suggestions.

MANAGEMENT

Management of the business is different from the production of the goods or delivery of the service. The skills involved here are those of marketing, finance, personnel and planning. Your business needs all of these skills to be successful. You may be planning to have a management team, but more likely the management of the business will consist entirely of you. Look at your past record of making things happen – refer back to your Look at Me! answers.

As you research this section you start to realise where the gaps are in terms of what is needed to manage your business. You will not be able to complete this section of the business plan until you have worked out how you will fill the gaps. It could be that you need some basic training in business management or particular aspects of running a business such as marketing. Business advisers can tell you what courses are available locally.

A gap you may not personally be able to fill still has to be closed. Look at alternatives – could you buy in management skills you need? For example, one woman set up her business to provide other businesses with a book-keeping service.

RESOURCES

What do you need to make your product or deliver your service? Itemise them, including staff, equipment and premises. You need staff with the skills to make or deliver your product/service. Once again, the skilled staff may be you! However, your practical skills may be rusty or you may not have the experience of working with the latest equipment. Plan how to improve your skills, if you need to. Check with your local college or the Job Centre to see whether Employment Training can offer training to develop the skills which you need.

Check out your needs for other resources such as premises and equipment. Do you already have items and space that you can use? If not, where will you find them and how much will they cost? Your answers form this section of the business plan. It is *essential* to know at this stage exactly how much your business will cost to start up and run at least for the first year. It is safe to assume that whatever you have forecast, it will take longer to become established and will cost more than you originally thought. So be very cautious and err on the side of pessimism.

FINANCE

This last section of the business plan is often known as the financial plan and tends to have an aura of mystique about it. Women often have an uncanny way of putting themselves down by saying 'oh I'm no good at figures', 'I could never do percentages'. This is patently a nonsense. Repeat the words as you read them, *I have successfully managed a household budget, therefore I can complete a financial plan and run the finances of my business.* You have to be able to write down, and therefore *know and understand* how much money the business needs, what the money is for, when the money is needed, where it will come from, and how you will control the flow of money in and out of your business. Once your business starts, by measuring the *actual* amount of cash coming in and out of the business (cashflow), against what you *said* would happen in the business plan, you will be able to see if things are going according to plan. If they are not, you can take immediate action to remedy the situation.

The words and terms used in financial planning may be unfamiliar, but their meanings are straightforward. Again, reading the booklets put out by the banks, the small firms service and the Enterprise Agencies will all help to increase your confidence in this area. Rhona appreciated that to be a medicinal herb supplier, she would have to lay out a large sum of money up front to buy stock. Money she did not have herself. Her ultimate business required a very small outlay of cash. She already had a computer and was able to work at home. She bought extra software, business stationery and a telephone answering machine, but did not need to buy anything else until she had won her first contract.

WHERE CAN YOU GET MONEY FROM?

Studies have shown that women have often felt themselves to be at a disadvantage when trying to raise money to start a business. So it is worth looking very carefully at how, and from whom, you might raise money. Have in your mind the sum you need. Finance comes in two ways – either as a loan, which needs to be repaid either with or without interest or as a grant – a sum of money *given* to you which does not have to be repaid.

SOURCES OF FINANCE
Your own savings or capital
Your family and friends
High street banks

Government (European, National & Local)
Venture Capitalists
Other sources

This list is by no means exhaustive and once again, the first port of call should be your Enterprise Agency/Trust. If you need to look for money outside the family they have the information to let you know what money may be available to you. There are many schemes all of which depend on certain factors such as your age, the kind of business you have (is it in the area of high technology, manufacturing?), whether you will be creating jobs, in which geographic location your business is situated and whether you have already started trading. Check out your eligibility before you start to trade. For example if you are under 25, the Prince's Youth Business Trust offers start-up grants. If you live or intend to start up a usiness in a coal or steel closure area, British Coal Enterprises or British Steel Enterprises could help finance your business. Many local authorities have small amounts of money, usually up to about £3000, that they will lend at low interest rates to new businesses. There are some schemes aimed specifically at women.

For example, Stirling District Council set up a special fund for women who were not eligible for the Enterprise Allowance Scheme. They make ten grants a year of £2000 to local women, on the basis of a sound business plan. This is in addition to their regular small start-up loan fund. Check with your local council to see what special schemes they have to help women into business. The European Community have small start-up grants available to encourage women to work together. The scheme is called the Local Employment Initiative (see the list of contact names at the end of this chapter).

YOUR OWN SAVINGS OR CAPITAL
You may already have enough cash and other resources to

start the business without having to go looking for money. However, many aspiring business-owners do not and women often find themselves without much money at all. What can you do? You may have a lump sum you can use, for example, money from redundancy, a legacy, or a pension. It is not wise, however, to depend solely on this money to fund the business. Other women have sold possessions or bought a smaller house and used the capital raised for the business. But women, especially, do find it difficult to use family money and possessions to finance their business. This is why it is *vital* to have the support of your family, because you will be asking them to make sacrifices too.

FAMILY AND FRIENDS

This is tricky. Some people would never dream of approaching family or friends for loans, yet they may be more than willing to lend you the money now when you need it rather than make you wait to inherit it later. In general, this is the cheapest way to borrow money. They may also wish to invest in your business and be 'sleeping partners'.

HIGH STREET BANKS

The banks are sources of loans, for start-up costs including capital purchases and also of overdraft facilities. But remember, an overdraft is not a loan. An overdraft enables you to keep writing cheques for materials, wages etc, to an agreed limit, even when you do not have the funds in your account to cover the cheques. This enables you to keep trading until your customers pay their bills. A loan is a sum of money repaid with interest over an agreed time.

Before a bank will give you a loan it will want to see some evidence of commitment to the business from you, that is how much of your own money you are putting in. It will certainly expect to see a business plan and may ask for some security in the form of your house or insurance policies, in the event of your not being able to pay back the loan.

If you have not had many dealings with the bank then the prospect of an interview to raise finance might seem very daunting. Let's put this into perspective. First of all, you are going to the bank to buy money, an item just like shoes or potatoes or a washing machine. You would not go into Curry's and be grateful to get the first thing they gave you. You would think about what you wanted the machine for, how much your budget was and on what terms you wanted to pay. You could then go to Comet, John Lewis and the rest before you made your decision.

Banks used to have reputations for trivialising women's businesses. One bank manager's comment, 'Go home and stick to your knitting' so enraged one older woman that she responded to the young male bank official with an icy 'I'll go home to my knitting when you go off to play with your train set'. But as more bank managers have interviewed more business women and realised that women are the fastest growing source of small business start-ups, so reports of being patronised or not taken seriously are fewer.

Developing a good working relationship with your bank is like developing one with your customers. Most banks are advertising their assistance to small businesses so take them up on their offers. Before the final version of your business plan is complete make an appointment to see someone at a branch specialising in dealing with business customers, and talk through your ideas and your plan. This will help you clear up any areas of uncertainty and get you used to the sort of questions normally asked at a business interview.

When the final plan is ready, make an appointment with the manager and tell him or her the purpose of the interview. Send a copy of your completed business plan in advance of the interview to give your bank manager a chance to read it.

GOVERNMENT

The Enterprise Allowance Scheme is the widely used Government measure to help unemployed people start up in business. If you qualify you will receive £80 per fortnight for a year. Sadly, many women do not qualify.

Key criteria that you must fulfil:

● Work full-time (36 hours or more per week in the business)
● Be receiving unemployment benefit or income support yourself or via a member of your family
● Have been unemployed for at least eight weeks
● Be between 18 and 65 years old
● Have access to £1000 (this could be an overdraft facility or loan)
● Have a business which is approved by the Department of Employment.

VENTURE CAPITAL

Venture Capital firms are institutions which are prepared to back business ventures when they are set up in exchange for a share in the company. They expect a rapid rate of company growth, a high return on their investment and usually sell their stake in the business after about five years. If you need a large financial investment in your business then make contact with them. You will find addresses at the end of the chapter. Your high street bank will also be able to help you.

COMPLETING THE FORMALITIES

At the same time as you are capturing your creative thoughts in your business plan, there are certain formal issues and legal aspects to running a business that you must consider.

These formalities may appear daunting, but take each item in turn and seek professional help if you need it. This chapter is not intended to be used as a reference book, but the following chart gives you the headings of the key areas that

COMPLETING THE FORMALITIES

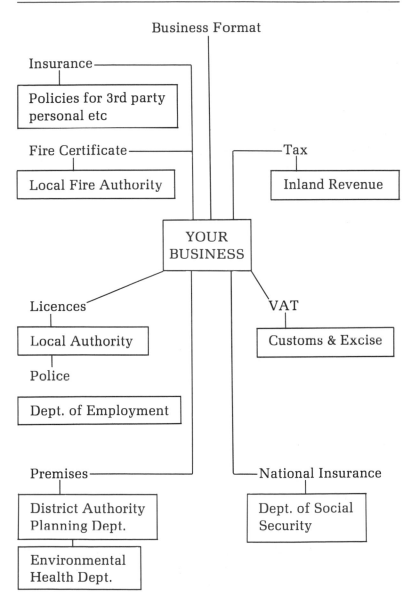

Business Format

Insurance

Policies for 3rd party personal etc

Fire Certificate

Local Fire Authority

Tax

Inland Revenue

YOUR BUSINESS

Licences

Local Authority

Police

Dept. of Employment

VAT

Customs & Excise

Premises

District Authority Planning Dept.

Environmental Health Dept.

National Insurance

Dept. of Social Security

2 3 3

you must look into. It is not meant to be an exhaustive list, but aims to show you those aspects of the law which apply to small businesses, and those government departments with which new businesses will have to deal. Not all of them may apply to your particular business. There are several good specialist books on this subject, but the best first stop is your local Enterprise Agency or Trust. They will advise you on any local regulations and may well have produced their own guide to the formalities.

Whatever you read and whoever you seek advice from, *do not sign anything without first seeing a lawyer*. A word-of-mouth recommendation from other satisfied business-owners is a good way to find a lawyer experienced in business law. One area in which you do have a choice, is that of business format.

THE BUSINESS FORMAT

The decision about what business format or structure to have may be an easy one to make. Indeed, the format – a part-nership or co-operative – may have been the deciding factor in wanting to start a business. If the decision is not obvious, then the following short guide to the ways in which you can trade may help you make up your mind. Also discuss it with your business adviser.

ON YOUR OWN – SOLE TRADER
This is the simplest and probably the most common form of doing business. It is easy to set up and you can trade under your own name or a business name. Your business is not dis-tinguished in any way from your personal affairs. This means that if your business fails then your creditors can seize your personal possessions to recover what you owe them. The income and business profits (after you deduct business expenses) are subject to income tax. You pay a flat-

rate, Class 2 National Insurance stamp as a sole trader, and Class 4 contribution on profits. There is no entitlement to unemployment benefit, industrial injury benefit or maternity benefit. When you die, the business dies with you. You may want to top-up your state pension entitlement by taking up a Personal Pension Plan. Check that your Pensions Adviser is a member of FIMBRA or LAUTRO.

PARTNERSHIP WITH OTHERS

A partnership is two or more self-employed people working together. Whatever holds good for a sole trader, holds good for a partnership. So you are responsible for the debts incurred by your partner, whether or not you knew he or she was running them up.

It does not matter how long you have known a potential partner, you must formalise your partnership in detail. Details such as how long a partner draws full wages if he or she is sick, are important. Do not start up in partnership, especially a family partnership, until you have signed a partnership agreement drawn up by a lawyer.

Partnerships can be very rewarding. Vicky and Margot set up their financial services business Money Counts when they both decided to leave their paid jobs.

For us there was a catalyst – our employer was giving us a rotten deal. If we'd accepted it we'd have been saying we weren't worth anything.

I would not have gone into business on my own, I'm a good seconder, a good organiser – but there has to be something to organise. I have drive and optimism and had enough faith in Margot's ideas to go for a business of our own. We believed in what we were doing and also that we were too good to work for anyone else.

We had known each other for 15 years but only started talking seriously four months before launching

> the business. We have a formal partnership agreement,
> but to make it work you have to be honest, talk openly
> and trust each other. It's a bit like a marriage, we play
> to each other's strengths, but in the end have to accept
> the total package. We rarely criticise each other – there
> are enough people out there doing it for you.
>   A partnership means you do not just jump into the
> deep end – your partner won't let you. The
> responsibility of running the business – we have a staff
> of 14 – can weigh heavily and keeping the enthusiasm
> alive is important. That's why having a partner is so
> vital, we shore each other up, give each other support.

LIMITED COMPANY

A limited company means that your business is an entity sep-
arate from yourself. A limited company needs a minimum of
two shareholders (for example, mother and daughter, wife
and husband, two friends), one director and a company secretary who could be a second director. Shareholders own the
business and directors run and manage it. In practice, these
can be the same people, but their functions are different.

The company itself has responsibility for its debts, not the
owners or directors (unless it can be proved that they ran the
business negligently). However, banks are unlikely to lend
money to a newly formed limited company without personal
guarantees from directors.

The owners or shareholders receive dividends out of profits; directors are paid a wage as they are employees of the
company. As an employee a director pays the usual rate of
National Insurance and is therefore entitled to claim all state
benefits. Talk to your business adviser about the implications, benefits and drawbacks about operating your business
as a limited company. Limited companies are fairly easy and
not too expensive to set up. You can buy a company 'off the
shelf' probably for less than £200. For this you will get, a

registered company with a name, the Memorandum and Articles of Association and the Certificate of Incorporation. These last items, essentially, are the 'rules' which state the nature of the business and how it will operate. Once again you need to decide how you want to allocate responsibilities within the firm, so that these 'rules' are written how you want.

A Company Registration Agent (which you can find in the Yellow Pages) will sell you an 'off the shelf' company, quickly and fairly painlessly, but in the first instance take advice from your lawyer or accountant. Your lawyer will also help set up a limited company for you, but it may cost you more. Once again sign nothing until you have consulted your lawyer.

CO-OPERATIVES

Here the workers are the owners of the business and the management style is democratic. You need a minimum of two members to form a co-operative and you establish the business for your benefit. You register the co-operative with the Registrar of Friendly Societies. It is important to contact your local co-operative development worker to help and advise you how to start up and manage the business.

FRANCHISES

Franchises are not actually a different form of doing business: a franchise can be operated by a sole trader, partnership or limited company. However, as more people, especially those with a sum of money to invest, are starting a business by taking up a franchise, it is worth looking at this type of business operation.

A franchise is an agreement whereby you, the franchisee, buy the right to use the name of another company and sell its products or services. Examples of franchises are Bodyshop, Wimpy, Kall-Kwik, Prontaprint.

The key organisations to advise you about franchising are the British Franchise Association (BFA) and the high street banks' Franchise Units. (See the end of the chapter for addresses.) Once more, do not sign anything until you have consulted a lawyer.

CONCLUSION

Examining your motives, generating ideas, doing market research, listening to advice, making decisions, writing the business plan are all vital to the process of planning a business. But however long and thoroughly you plan, however much support you have, there is a moment when you have to say, now is the time, my business starts today, and begin!

We always say to our would-be business-owners 'Have you got the get up and go to get up and go?' You may have seen the television programmes, you have now read this book. If, like Rhona, you want to run your own show your own way then get up and go . . . and good luck!

FURTHER INFORMATION

USEFUL ADDRESSES

ORGANISATIONS OF SPECIAL INTEREST TO WOMEN

INDUSTRIAL COMMON OWNERSHIP MOVEMENT (ICOM)
Women's Link-up, c/o Vassalli House, 20 Central Road, Leeds LS1 6DE
Tel: (0532) 461737/8

WOMEN IN ENTERPRISE
26 Bond Street, Wakefield WF7 2QP
Tel: (0924) 361789
WOMEN'S ENTERPRISE DEVELOPMENT AGENCY (WEDA)
Aston Science Park, Love Lane, Aston Triangle,
Birmingham B7 4BJ
Tel: (021) 359 0178   Contact: Anna Douglas
WOMEN'S ENTERPRISE UNIT
Scottish Enterprise Foundation, University of Stirling,
Stirling FK9 4LA
Tel: (0786) 73171   Contact: Christina Hartshorn
WOMEN'S LOCAL EMPLOYMENT INITIATIVES
CEI, 42 Frederick Street, Edinburgh EH2 1EX
Tel: (031) 225 3144   Contact: Alicia Bruce
WOMEN'S LOCAL EMPLOYMENT INITIATIVES
Birmingham City Council, 110 Colmore Row, Birmingham
B3 3AG
Tel: (021) 236 4441

OTHER ORGANISATIONS
ASSOCIATION OF BRITISH CHAMBERS OF COMMERCE
212a Shaftesbury Avenue, London WC2H 8EW
Tel: (071) 140 5831
BRITISH FRANCHISE ASSOCIATION
Thames View, New Town Road, Henley-on-Thames, Oxon
RG9 1HG Oxon
Tel: (0491) 578049
BUSINESS IN THE COMMUNITY (BIC)
227a City Road, London EC1V 1JU
Tel: (071) 253 3716
Note: BIC will be able to provide you with the name and
address of your local Enterprise Agency
COMPANIES REGISTRATION OFFICE
Companies House, 55 City Road, London EC1Y 1BB
Tel: (071) 253 9393

NATIONAL FEDERATION OF SELF-EMPLOYED & SMALL BUSINESSES
Head Office NFSE & SB Ltd, 32 St Ann's Road West, Lytham St Anns, Lancashire FY8 1NY
Tel: (0253) 720911
RURAL DEVELOPMENT COMMISSION
141 Castle Street, Salisbury SP1 3TP
Tel: (0722) 336255
Note: The RDA has offices throughout the country
SMALL FIRMS SERVICE
Tel: 100 and ask for Freephone Enterprise

VENTURE CAPITAL
VENTURE CAPITAL ASSOCIATION
3 Catherine Place, London SW1E 6DX
Tel: (071) 233 5212

**LOCAL ORGANISATIONS –
IN NORTHERN IRELAND**
ENTERPRISE NORTHERN IRELAND
Crescent House, 14 High Street, Holywood, County Down BT18 9AZ
Tel: (02317) 7646
Please mark all correspondence 'Enterprise Northern Ireland'.
NORTHERN IRELAND CO-OPERATIVE DEVELOPMENT AGENCY
Canada House, 22 North Street, Belfast BT1 1LA
Tel: (0232) 232755
NORTHERN IRELAND SMALL BUSINESS INSTITUTE
BP Enterprise House, University of Ulster at Jordanstown, Shore Road, Newtonabbey BT37 0QB
Tel: (0232) 365060

LOCAL ORGANISATIONS – IN SCOTLAND
REGISTER OF COMPANIES FOR SCOTLAND
102 George Street, Edinburgh EH2 3DJ
Tel: (031) 225 5774

SCOTTISH BUSINESS IN THE COMMUNITY (SCOTBIC)
Romano House, 43 Station Road, Corstorphine, Edinburgh
EH12 7AF
Tel: (031) 334 9876
Note: SCOTBIC can give you the name and address of your
local Enterprise Trust
SCOTTISH CO-OPERATIVES DEVELOPMENT COMMITTEE LTD (SCDC)
Templeton Business Centre, Templeton Street, Bridgeton,
Glasgow G40 1DA
Tel: (041) 554 3797
SCOTTISH DEVELOPMENT AGENCY
Rosebery House, Haymarket Terrace, Edinburgh
EH12 5EZ
Tel: (031) 337 9595

LOCAL ORGANISATIONS – IN WALES
DEVELOPMENT BOARD FOR RURAL WALES
Ladywell House, Newton, Powys SY16 1JB
Tel: (0686) 626965
WALES CO-OPERATIVE DEVELOPMENT AND TRAINING CENTRE
Llandaff Court, Fairwater Road, Cardiff CF5 2XP
Tel: (0222) 554955
THE WELSH DEVELOPMENT AGENCY
Business Centre, Triangle Park, Pentrebach, Merthyr
Tydfil, Mid Glamorgan, CF48 4YB
Tel: (0685) 722177

USEFUL BOOKS

- *The Business Plan Workbook*, Colin and Paul Barrow,
  Kogan Page
- *Do Your Own Market Research*, Paul Hague and Peter
  Jackson, Kogan Page
- *The Greatest Little Business Book*, Peter Hingston,
  Hingston
- *Ideas Generation Workbook*, Pat Richardson and

Laurence Clarke, Scottish Enterprise Foundation
Note: Available by post from Scottish Enterprise
Foundation, University of Stirling, Stirling, price £2.40
- *Law for the Small Business*, Patricia Clayton, Kogan
  Page
- *Presenting a Business Plan*, Ernst & Young
- *Starting and Running Your Own Business*, Dennis
  Millar, Department of Employment
- *Starting a Successful Small Business*, M. J. Morris,
  Kogan Page

GENERAL BOOKS FOR WOMEN RETURNERS

- *Back to Work*, Gemma O'Connor, MacDonald Optima
- *Hours to Suit*, Anna Alston and Ruth Miller, Rooters
- *Making a Comeback*, Margaret Korving, Hutchinson
- *Managing Two Careers*, Patricia O'Brien, Sheldon Press
- *Returning to Work: A Practical Guide for Women*, Alec
  Reed, Kogan Page, 1989
- *Returning to Work Handbook*, Good Housekeeping
- *Women Can Achieve Career Success*, Maggie Steel and
  Zita Thornton, Grapevine
- *Women Can Return to Work*, Maggie Steel and Zita
  Thornton, Grapevine, 1988
- *Women Working It Out*, Jane Chapman, COIC, 1987
- *Working Mother: A Practical Handbook*, Marianne
  Velmans and Sarah Litrinoff, Corgi

Waterstones
5-99

WOMEN
MEAN
BUSINESS

BBC BOOKS

ACKNOWLEDGEMENTS

We would like to thank *all* the people who helped us produce this book. We are especially grateful to the women we talked to and interviewed, who have allowed us to tell their stories, and to our colleagues and friends who helped with ideas, advice and encouragement.

We are also grateful to our editors at BBC Books – without whom this book would not have been possible.

For our mothers – both women returners

Published by BBC Books,
a division of BBC Enterprises Limited,
Woodlands, 80 Wood Lane, London W12 0TT

First published 1991
© Caroline Bamford and Catherine McCarthy 1991

ISBN 0 563 36092 5

Designed by Peter Bridgewater
Illustrations by Martin Shovel

Set in 10½/13 Melior Roman by Ace Filmsetting Ltd, Frome
Printed and bound in Great Britain by Clays Ltd, St Ives Plc
Cover printed by Clays Ltd, St Ives Plc